Modern Sniper Rifles

DUNCAN LONG

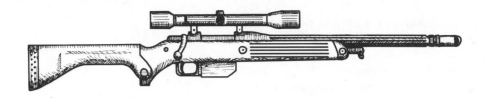

Modern Sniper Rifles

DUNCAN LONG

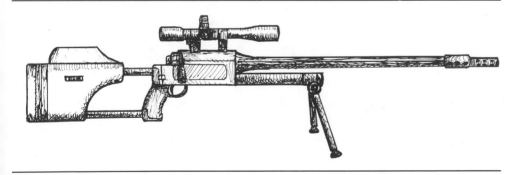

PALADIN PRESS
BOULDER, COLORADO

Also by Duncan Long:

AK47: The Complete Kalashnikov Family of Assault Rifles
AR-7 Super Systems
The AR-15/M16: A Practical Guide
AR-15/M16 Super Systems
Assault Pistols, Rifles, and Submachine Guns
Automatics: Fast Firepower, Tactical Superiority
Combat Ammunition: Everything You Need to Know
Combat Revolvers: The Best (and Worst) Modern Wheelguns
Combat Rifles of the 21st Century: Futuristic Firearms
   for Tomorrow's Battlefields
Firearms for Survival
The Mini-14: The Plinker, Hunter, Assault, and Everything Else Rifle
Modern Ballistic Armor: Clothing, Bomb Blankets, Shields,
   Vehicle Protection . . . Everything You Need to Know
Powerhouse Pistols: The Colt 1911 and Browning Hi-Power Sourcebook
The Ruger .22 Automatic Pistol: Standard/Mark I/Mark II Series
Streetsweepers: The Complete Book of Combat Shotguns
The Sturm, Ruger 10/22 Rifle and .44 Magnum Carbine
The Terrifying Three: Uzi, Ingram, and Intratec Weapons Families

Modern Sniper Rifles
by Duncan Long
Copyright © 1988 by Duncan Long

ISBN 0-87364-470-0
Printed in the United States of America

Published by Paladin Press, a division of
Paladin Enterprises, Inc., P.O. Box 1307,
Boulder, Colorado 80306, USA.
(303) 443-7250

Direct inquiries and/or orders to the above address.

CONTENTS

WARNING

Technical data presented here, particularly concerning ammunition and the use, adjustment, and alteration of firearms, inevitably reflects the author's individual beliefs and experience with particular firearms, equipment, and components under specific circumstances which the reader cannot duplicate exactly. The information in this book should therefore be used for guidance only and the information approached with great caution. Neither the author nor the publisher assumes any responsibility for the use or misuse of information contained in this book.

ACKNOWLEDGMENTS

Thanks must go to the many companies which so graciously loaned firearms, accessories, and equipment to me to test out during the writing of this book as well as furnishing photographs and hard-to-find information and history about their products. A big thank you should also go to the fine people at Paladin Press, and to Peder Lund for masterminding the idea for this book. Thanks must also go to Maggie, Kristen, and Nicholas for keeping things quiet on the home front.

1

Sniper Rifle History

Mankind's very first battles undoubtedly took place within arm's reach as combatants used sticks, stones, or whatever objects were at hand. With the development of such weapons as spears and bows and arrows, fighters most likely began to use crude methods of camouflage and concealment to ambush enemies. Early man undoubtedly learned quickly that with proper tactics, a bow man or rock thrower on high ground could harass or even overcome an enemy who had superior numbers and greater armament but lacked the wisdom to deploy them to proper advantage.

This ability to use tactics and weapons skill to overcome superior forces is what sniping is all about. The sniper must use his wits rather than meet the enemy head-on, where overwhelming numbers of soldiers and amounts of armament decide the outcome of the battle. Throughout history, the sniper has short-circuited the normal course of a battle by cutting down leaders or destroying important equipment. For the sniper, precision takes the place of massive firepower and random destruction.

With the development of the "professional" soldier and improvements in firearms during the European Industrial Revolution, the ability of one man to derail the "normal" flow of battle has been seen by military leaders as "unsporting." Chivalry, rules of conduct, "gentlemanly behavior," conventions of war, and the like were conjured up in an effort to blacken the reputation of anyone who might even think about the use of snipers in battle.

Tacticians feel a great need to keep things orderly on the battlefield. In the past, troops marched into battle in neat little rows and military leaders made use of exposed, geometric maneuver formations. Modern strategists still deal with maps full of pins and displays of force positions, ever striving to make order out of the chaos of war. Even with the introduction of heavy artillery and machine guns, commanders still used massed, synchronized charges across open fields devoid of obstacles to overwhelm an enemy with the sheer mass of men.

In such conditions, the use of snipers to cut down leaders or key personnel could throw things into even greater confusion. The idea of cutting down the "professionals" while the little men who were supposed to be sacrificing their lives for their countries remained unscathed certainly did little to make the sniper admired by military leaders. It is little wonder, then, that armies using snipers were often painted as being barbaric while snipers themselves, if captured, were often executed on the spot.

Despite the animosity toward snipers, they continued to be used by those more interested in winning wars than in obeying the rules of chivalry. By the time of the U.S. Civil War, both sides were employing snipers with deadly results. (According to the writings of the time, special marksmen using Sharps .52-caliber buffalo rifles were able to strike an enemy soldier up to a mile away.)

The East has been more willing to deploy large numbers of snipers in its armies; Western armies have been slower in the learning of the lessons of history. The use of snipers by the Germans in World War II and later in Finland during the Soviet invasion of that country taught a lesson to Kremlin military planners that has been taken to heart. Most Western military forces, however, still suffer from minor aversions to the use of snipers, as well as basic misunderstandings of how to use them.

The United States is no exception. A good indication of this lack of tactical understanding in the use of snipers is shown in the types of weapons which have been used for U.S. sniper rifles. Fewer than ten types of rifles have ever been designated and adopted as sniper rifles by the U.S. Army or Marine Corps (those only after the beginning of World War I). Furthermore, most of these were actually standard military rifles which were modified by mounting an often fragile sporting scope. The few exceptions to this (such as the Sharps buffalo rifles used during the Civil War or the M40 the Marines currently use) are actually modified sporters. The U.S. military has never actually adopted a weapon designed specifically for sniper use, instead modifying a rifle to create a make-do weapon.

Sniper use by the U.S. military has also often reflected a lack of understanding of the sniper's full potential. During World War I, snipers were deployed by the Americans only after it was realized that the "stray shots" that were killing a disproportionate number of military officers were actually sniper fire. Even then, sniper training was nearly nonexistent. With the close of World War I, all thought of training snipers was again abandoned by the U.S. military.

As in World War I, snipers were deployed during World War II and in the Korean War only after enemy troops were found to be using snipers. The weapons used then—the M1C and M1D—were simply Garand rifles equipped with 4-power scopes originally made for use on hunting rifles.

When the U.S. adopted the powerful M14 for its infantry rifle as the war in Indochina was heating up, the designation "sniper" was actually officially deleted from the Army's nomenclature and the idea of using snipers completely abandoned! Only after U.S. troops faced the effective use of snipers by communist forces in Vietnam did the U.S. military dust off its Army Marksmanship Training Unit sniper work to reestablish a sniper curriculum in the late 1960s. Following the practice of using the standard rifle as a sniper rifle (and despite a considerable amount of bureaucratic research and testing of a number of experimental rifles), the M14 was finally adopted as the new sniper weapon.

Fortunately, the M14 rifle—designated the M21 in its sniper guise—could be rebuilt by Army armorers so that it had minute-of-angle or better accuracy. Rather than use a standard sporting scope for the new sniper rifle, Redfield 3- to 9-power variable scopes were modified according to a system developed by Captain James Leatherwood; they could then automatically determine range and compensate for the bullet's ballistic drop.

While it appeared that the U.S. was finally going to have a useful sniper rifle in its arsenal and make good use of snipers, only a few of the effective M21 rifles were ever actually made or ever deployed in Vietnam.

Snipers in Vietnam were misused. During the late 1960s when the U.S. sniper program was finally started in earnest, snipers were often used by commanders as squad leaders, and many were killed in battle after being ordered to assault positions or when walking point during patrols. In effect, the sniper was treated as just another foot soldier.

The few snipers that were properly used in Vietnam proved that modern sniper rifles could be devastatingly effective. In the "high-tech" war, where the average cost of killing an enemy soldier often ran into the thousands of dollars, the killing done by snipers proved to be very cheap thanks to one-shot kills. During a seven-month period in 1969, Army snipers managed to kill 1,245 Viet Cong with an average of 1.39 rounds expended per kill.

Strangely enough, much of the sniping work engaged in by the U.S. forces in Vietnam resulted from programs developed by both the CIA and the Special Forces in an effort to use new techniques of psychological warfare and clandestine methods of attacking the North Vietnamese as well as the Viet Cong. Many of these tactics made use of sniper rifles, which were often equipped with silencers.

Since the military was being pressed to develop various weapons, and since the theory and design of silencers had never before been promoted by the U.S. military, private industry started marketing commercially made sniper systems as well as silencer units capable of being used on military rifles.

Perhaps the best known of these commercial undertakings was that of Military Armaments

Corporation, which was run by Mitcheil Livingston WerBel III. Many of its firearms and silencers worked very effectively and were soon being used as sniper rifles during raids conducted by Special Forces, SEAL teams, and the CIA in Vietnam (and possibly in surrounding countries).

During the early 1960s, when the U.S. military was still trying to decide what rifle to designate as its sniper weapon, "field-expedient" sniper rifles were being created by U.S troops in the field. One of the more common of these, especially in special operations, was the use of the M16 rifle—often equipped with a silencer. Also common, especially in the hands of Marine snipers, were Winchester Model 70 bolt-action rifles fitted with sporter scopes (interestingly, the U.S. Marines later selected another sporter—the Remington 700 with a heavy varmint barrel—as the basis of its current sniper rifle).

At the end of the Vietnam War, much of the U.S. military's interest in sniper rifles again waned. At the time of this writing, however, it appears that development of rapid-deployment forces to combat small brush wars and the threat of large-scale terrorism has kept interest in sniper rifles alive in some military circles. The fact that the Soviet Union and other communist countries have large sniper programs has undoubtedly caused many U.S. military leaders to become interested in sniper programs as well.

Sniper rifles are also found in the hands of law-enforcement personnel as political unrest, increased crime, and the rise in terrorism create a need for sniper rifles among law-enforcement authorities and special teams created to deal with such problems. Those dealing with terrorists have found that, while storming buildings (or even using artillery or bombs) is not practical, a precise shot by a sniper is capable of removing a terrorist with surgical precision while leaving hostages unharmed.

Unfortunately, though the West has finally started developing sniper programs to deal with crime and for use in war, American society still attaches a stigma to the term "sniper." Many segments of the press, as well as the general population, feel that killing a criminal to keep him from harming a victim is somehow too harsh. The press is not always favorable to police or military snipers who actually save hostages. Also, some segments of the press feed the public a subliminal message that snipers are bad just by using the word "sniper" for those individuals who, on rare occasions, go on shooting sprees, killing people from rooftops. Such cold-blooded "snipers" can then be associated with police or military snipers in the mind of the average man on the street.

Fictional TV shows and movies also tarnish the image of the sniper. It was recently disclosed that censors on one of the major TV networks have a policy in which the "good guys" in police shows must always give the bad guy a chance to shoot first and must always meet him head on; these programs cause many viewers to think that the police should not fire until a criminal fires first, even if the criminal has a weapon and is obviously about to use it to harm someone. (According to noted writer Massad Ayoob, who's often called to be an expert witness in police cases, policemen have been alarmed recently when jurists have argued that a policeman was guilty of using unreasonable force when he shot a criminal rather than just shooting the firearm out of the criminal's hand!)

In the real world, snipers can't save a hostage by waiting until things get out of hand and a criminal or terrorist actually starts shooting—and killing—people.

One way that is being used to combat the negative image of the sniper is to avoid using the word "sniper." Police snipers are now called "marksmen" or "counter-snipers" (if the public views snipers as bad guys, then counter-snipers are the good guys). Likewise, those selling sniper rifles advertise them as "special-purpose" rifles, and not all of the "match" and "target" rifles being sold these days are ending up in the hands of sport shooters.

No doubt another reason for the negative attitude toward snipers has to do with the fact that a special type of person is needed to wield a sniper rifle. With the use of optics, the sniper often actually sees his opponent (which usually isn't the case in modern warfare, where an enemy is obscured by smoke, terrain, and/or camouflage on the battlefield and, when seen, is seen only fleetingly). To be capable of making such personal kills takes a strong and special type of personality. Such a person must be committed emotionally and mentally to the moral correctness of what he is doing and believe in the battle being waged against his enemy. Such a man must also be capable of living with himself afterward, sorting out his feelings of right and wrong without carrying disabling emotional baggage. Few people are capable of such emotional and mental control and self-assurance. In the eyes of the many, the sniper is a breed apart.

Snipers are, by virtue of their nature and negative attitude of the public, cautious about telling others of their experiences. Thus, a lot of "tall tales" about snipers and their exploits have emerged to fill the vacuum, which also paint the sniper as a half-human, heartless individual. Of course, such stories do little to help the sniper's image.

Trends

There are a number of super-precise rifles and new innovations in scopes designed for sniper use. With the development of new sniper rifles come eight sometimes divergent trends which may lead to a number of different sniper weapons in the near future.

One trend is the creation of "high-tech" rifles using new alloys and plastics. In addition to creating less expensive and more weather-resistant rifles, such guns may become lighter and more accurate than their current counterparts. The use of computer designing techniques and robot-controlled machinery also promises the marketing of small runs of sniper rifles which might not otherwise be produced due to the relatively small market for such weapons.

The second trend is toward semiauto sniper rifles rather than bolt-action guns. The USSR, Warsaw Block, and China have already made the switch to such rifles (most of which are based on the AK-47 action), and only a few militaries in the West still use bolt-action rifles. As the semiauto military rifle becomes ever more accurate, it is doubtful that the bolt-action rifle will remain in use for long, even as a sniper weapon.

(With police officers using sniper rifles, this trend does not seem as evident, since quality sporting and target rifles like the Ruger M77, Winchester 70, and Remington 700 are still the most common guns in use. There are a few inroads being made into this segment of the sniping market by semiauto versions of military rifles, however, especially with the Colt AR-15 series of rifles.)

A third possible trend, if the tendency to use target/match rifles for the basis of sniper weapons is any indication, will be the occasional use of "handguns" as sniper weapons. While such use may now seem farfetched to most of us, pistols currently in production (like the Thompson/Center Contender) are capable of great accuracy. They could be used as a sniper weapon in the hands of a skilled shooter, especially in the short ranges encountered in many urban areas.

Compared to a rifle, a "sniper pistol" is lightweight, easily carried, and easily concealed. Such a weapon would be ideal for special purposes, and the soldier or policeman carrying it would hardly appear extraordinary until he put down his service weapon and pulled out his scoped sniper pistol.

While the 500- to 1,000-yard sniper shot occurs on occasion, recent studies by the FBI have found that most shots fired by police riflemen are taken at around 50 yards (with 76 yards being the average). Military snipers are believed to generally engage targets within 300 yards, with shots under 100 yards probably being most common. Such statistics make the idea of a sniper pistol seem practical.

The short range of the average sniper shot has created the trend toward less powerful cartridges in sniper rifles, with the .223 Remington (5.56mm NATO) chosen more and more over the more powerful .30-caliber chamberings. In fact, scoped carbines chambered for the 9mm Luger are occasionally being pressed into service as sniper rifles, and there has even been serious talk of using .22 rifles (perhaps equipped with silencers) for some types of sniper work. While some may argue that these small rounds are inadequate for sniper use, the move toward less powerful cartridges continues nevertheless.

The use of smaller, less powerful cartridges and lighter rifles has itself created a contradictory trend toward heavier rifles and larger calibers, with some snipers now finding themselves carrying heavy rifles (often weighing in at twenty or more pounds) and firing magnum sporting cartridges (like the 7mm Magnum, .338 Magnum, or even modified .50-caliber machine gun ammunition). These large sniper weapons fill a niche being left by the smaller guns since their larger chambers are capable of hitting targets over a mile away. These rifles also have the potential of being pitted against machines and equipment as well as against human targets (airplanes, computers, and other relatively fragile equipment are becoming the new targets for tomorrow's sniper). Super-sniper rifles deployed with devastating results over long distances will turn the sniper into a long-range saboteur.

The sixth trend is toward the use of special muzzle brakes (especially with the large-caliber sniper rifles) or silencers. These devices enable snipers to have greater control over their weapons and, in the case of the silencer, even help conceal the sniper's position. While silencers are not totally efficient at hiding the muzzle noise of a high-power rifle or capable of stopping the crack of the bullet as it breaks the sound barrier, they do confuse an enemy since it is nearly impossible to pinpoint a sniper's position from one hundred yards or more based on the muzzle sound from his shot.

The seventh trend is toward scopes which have been designed specifically for sniper use (as opposed to using sporting scopes). Such scopes have many features not found on sporter scopes and usually have the capability of compensating more accurately for bullet drop and range-estimating qualities. These scopes are also becoming more rugged since the conditions under which they will be used are often more adverse than those faced by sporting optics.

The final trend is toward greater accuracy, to a degree unheard of just a few decades ago. This accuracy comes about from improvements in barrel making, gunsmithing, optical systems, and ammunition. While sniper rifles having the accuracy of 2 MOA (Minutes of Action) were considered very accurate in the mid-1900s, sniper rifles of today often exhibit accuracy of 1 to 1/2 MOA. Many off-the-shelf military rifles can be made into good sniper rifles by simply mounting a scope on them. (U.S. military trainers, for example, have discovered that the new M16A2—without modification—is capable of accuracy achieved only with M14 rifles specifically reworked by armorers for rifle team competition.)

When one stops to think about the accuracy possible with a rifle shooting 1/2 MOA, it almost defies belief. Since half an MOA translates to roughly a half-inch group at one hundred yards, a skilled sniper with a quality rifle and scope could place his bullets within a three-inch circle at 500 yards. Where previous generations of snipers were capable of making head shots at 200 yards, the current sniper can just as easily shoot his opponent in the eye from a considerably greater distance. (One has to wonder what type of accuracy may be possible in the near future. The current joke that the next generation of sniper rifles will enable a sniper to hit his opponent through a keyhole may not be far from the truth!)

And what about future trends?

For the foot soldier of tomorrow, the trend seems to be toward military rifles which shoot bursts of projectiles rather than single, accurately fired shots.

This comes about because, on the modern battlefield, an enemy is seldom seen; when seen, it is for only a few moments. Shooting, therefore, is practically at random, with little time for aiming.

It would seem ironic that as assault rifles become accurate enough to be used as sniper rifles with the mere addition of a scope, firearms designers will be creating weapons which disperse shots into a pattern on and around a target (rather than being capable of accurately placing a single shot on target.) This may mean that the current generation of assault rifles will become the "special-purpose" sniper rifles of tomorrow, while the average soldier carries a weapon which fires caseless ammunition in fast bursts or fires single rounds filled with shot or flechettes.

As new sniper weapons of the far future replace the "old" assault rifle/sniper guns of today, they will become more and more radical, with new metal and glass fibers being used in conjunction with strong plastic and ceramics to create nonmetal barrels and receivers. These materials could drop the weight of a firearm to the point where the "heavy-barrel" sniper rifle of tomorrow might weigh in at four or five pounds rather than the ten to fifteen pounds of today.

Perhaps the most radical changes in sniper rifles will come about with new research in the area of superconductivity. Because today's electrical components and wiring offer high resistance to the conduction of electricity, a lot of power is converted into heat and wasted when "pushing" electrons through circuitry. Some superconducting metals are currently available, but they need very low temperatures in which to operate. That could change if current work toward creating room temperature superconducting metals succeeds.

Many physicists are talking of such a breakthrough occurring in the late 1980s or early 1990s, and small amounts of superconducting metals appear to have already been created (though the exact mechanism/theory of how small amounts of the superconductors were created is still a laboratory mystery, making it hard to duplicate the process).

Should superconductor metals become readily available in the near future, small, powerful motors and super computers which need little current would also become possible. For the sniper, this would mean that "smart scopes" with very powerful miniature computers built into them would become practical to manufacture. Such scopes would be capable of automatically figuring the range to the target, calculating ballistic arcs, and adjusting the scope in a fraction of a second. The scope itself might be optically connected to a helmet display, making it unnecessary for the sniper to shoulder his weapon; he could fire from the hip or from a position where only the scope and muzzle of his weapon were exposed to enemy view. The scope itself might "see" in the infrared/ultraviolet ranges and could have an IFF (Identification, Friend or Foe) system to ensure that targets weren't actually friendlies. The scope might even scan for enemies on the battlefield and alert the sniper as to their location.

The sniper could also have a "smart" helmet equipped with a night-vision visor capable of seeing in the infrared range. The "bullet-proof" helmet could remain lightweight while incorporating sensors which would give the wearer the ability to detect foes to his sides and behind him. The sniper of the future may literally have electronic eyes in the back of his head and might wear a ballistic armor suit which automatically changed its color to suit his surroundings. It will probably have warning displays inside the helmet's visor to warn the user of chemical, biological, or nuclear weapons or other hazards of the battlefield. The suit will probably be computerized and might even converse with the sniper.

Because superconductive metals could reduce the size and amount of electricity needed by a motor by up to 90 percent, gyroscopes mounted on a sniper rifle would also become a practical possibility. These gyrostabilizers, coupled to the smart scope, would allow the sniper to lock onto a moving target or even fire his rifle while running. The need to fire from a stationary position could be a thing of the past!

Superconductivity would also allow motors to be added to the barrel or stock so that under the smart scope's guidance, the rifle could actually track targets; there is even serious talk among weapons designers of a soldier's rifle being attached to his suit and aimed automatically from a helmet display. Through the use of a computer target-acquisition system, the sniper might be able to use a "burst mode" to engage multiple targets. Where a sniper

once had to choose the most important target, he might be able to take out a whole squad of men before the sound of his first shot reached their ears.

It is also possible that the sniper of tomorrow won't be limited to human targets and lightly armored vehicles and equipment if small, hand-held railguns become practical.

Railguns are a relatively new way of propelling projectiles. They work by creating an intense magnetic field between two metal rails. The magnetic field propels a shell along it to speed out the front of the rails. Where bullets of today travel around 3,000 fps (feet per second), rail guns can propel projectiles at 40,000 fps or more with trajectories being basically straight lines. The speed of a railgun will make bullet drop compensation and windage irrelevant for most targets that can be readily seen by the human eye. The power created by the high-speed velocity will allow small projectiles to easily penetrate even the heavy armor of tanks or concrete bunkers. Hand-held railguns would make tanks and low flying aircraft obsolete from the field of battle.

While current railguns are monstrous affairs that take large amounts of energy to work, superconductive metals could miniaturize these weapons to handheld proportions. Work is also being done on magnetic coil systems which, with superconductive metals, might also be capable of producing speeds rivaling that of the railgun in hand-held weapons.

Even the human sniper may no longer be on the battlefield in the far future thanks to current work on robotic fighters which will travel across battlefields, oblivious to the dangers of chemical, biological, or nuclear weapons. The whole shape of the future battlefield is hard to imagine, and just how many of these projections will become reality remains to be seen.

In the meantime, it is a certainty that snipers and sniper rifles are here to stay, especially as the West realizes the need to counter the widespread use of snipers by Communist countries and as civilized countries worldwide realize the need for "marksmen" to combat crime and terrorism. The need for the precision which only a sniper is capable of is greater today than ever before.

2

Ammunition

Although little ammunition is actually manufactured for the "sniper market," commercial sporting ammunition has a wide array of rounds suitable for sniper use, and a number of military "match" rounds are also ideal for many sniper applications. (The exception to sporter/match availability is for those snipers who have opted for .50-caliber rifles or the like. Such shooters will generally have to reload their own ammunition or use rounds designed for the .50-caliber Browning machine gun.)

Despite the availability of commercial and military ammunition, many snipers reload to wring out the last bit of accuracy from their rifle. Reloading also makes it possible to create special-purpose ammunition not otherwise available. Care should be taken when reloading sniper rounds, especially those used by police snipers, and some thought must be given to the public outcry which might result if the press decided that "killer" bullets had been created by the sniper to "do in" a poor, misguided criminal. Likewise, a military sniper might be in hot water if he were captured with expanding ammunition in his weapon. (For those who are interested in reloading special-purpose ammunition such as armor-piercing rounds, safety slugs, and subsonic loads, see my book *Combat Ammunition* for a look at the various techniques used in producing such ammunition.)

Currently, reloading for cheap practice doesn't make much sense if the sniper's time is worth anything at all, since companies like Winchester (with its inexpensive USA line), Federal Cartridge Company (with its American Eagle ammunition), and PMC (with its military-style, Korean-made ammunition) offer quality ammunition in large lots for nearly as little as it costs for the components to reload the ammunition. The time saved in buying manufactured ammunition for the sniper is better spent in practice shooting rather than honing skills at pumping a reloading press. As to accuracy, all the major companies offer quality match-type ammunition which is extremely accurate—usually more accurate than loads created by reloaders (one excellent example is Federal Cartridge's Match ammunition). Likewise, those with access to military "match" ammunition will find it more accurate than most shooter's reloads.

For maximum accuracy with any type of ammunition (including military), it is important to use ammunition from the same case lots rather than mixing ammunition from different runs. It is also beneficial to weigh each round if the sniper has access to very sensitive scales. Since there is a chance of encountering a round which has a low weight for one component and a high weight for another in the same shell, the scales will often alert the user to a round which is slightly different from the others. While rounds which are too heavy or too light are very rare with the commercial manufacturers listed above, they do sometimes occur; removing such rounds from a group can keep out the "fliers" from sniping ammunition.

Snipers need to do maximum damage with each shot fired. Greatest lethality is usually obtained from ammunition topped with soft-point Spitzer bullets. If used over the longer ranges of the round, boat-tail bullets may also help out both in accuracy and in giving slightly greater velocity at longer ranges. (Nonmilitary snipers using the new AR-15A2 or other .223 rifles with fast-twist barrels may also wish to try out the new SS109/M855 round in their rifle. The round has very good ballistics which may make it ideal for some types of sniper use; it has the ability to penetrate thin armor and still break apart to create extensive wounds when hitting flesh and blood. The civilian counterpart to this round is currently available from the Hansen Cartridge Company.)

Finding the most accurate round for any given rifle is a matter of experimentation. Factors to consider include the brand of ammunition, best weight, and style of bullet. The wise sniper will obtain a number of boxes of all types of ammunition available to him and go to the rifle range to determine which works best in his weapon. If the sniper may be called upon to use his rifle at night, night-time testing of various types of ammunition is also important to determine which type produces minimum muzzle flash.

There's a lot of controversy as to which chambering is best for sniper use. Some shooters bad-mouth larger rounds as being too powerful or having excessive recoil while the smaller rounds are viewed by some as fit only for hunting crippled woodchucks. Fortunately, both extremes are inaccurate, and most chamberings found for sniper rifles are suitable because they are useful in many situations in which they will be used.

In general, the chambering selected should be decided on the basis of what is needed in the way of performance and the distance over which the sniper will be firing. Those who wish to use bolt-action rifles have a wide range of sporter-style rifles from which to choose as the basis of a sniper rifle, with rounds like the .25-06, .270 Winchester, and .30-06 all being available; a little study of ballistic tables will often reveal the weaknesses and strengths of these rounds for various types of sniper use. Those who choose a semiauto sniper rifle will find themselves limited for the most part to military rounds and their sporter spin-offs.

Among the newer military rounds, the .223/ 5.56mm round is proving to have a lot going for it, especially within the 300 yards in which most

sniping occurs. For those who must use FMJ (full-metal jacket) ammunition due to the conventions of war (which ban all soft points, hollow points, pure-lead bullets, and poisoned bullets), the .223 is actually superior to the 7.62mm NATO/.308 Winchester. The larger round doesn't tumble within a human being in time to do maximum damage; in contrast, the .223 bullet will tumble upon hitting flesh and blood to create massive damage. With the new faster twists (1 twist per 10 inches of barrel, 1-in-9, and especially 1-in-7), the .223 FMJ will actually break apart upon entering a human being. These multiple projectiles each create extensive damage so that the wound created by the .223 FMJ bullet often mimics that of an expanding bullet. Expanding bullets create even more damage in the .223, especially with the slower 1-in-12 and 1-in-14 twists.

In .223 sniper rifles with a 1-in-12 twist, the 52 and 53 hollow points get peak accuracy, with other hollow points following close behind (though the standard 55-grain Spitzer ammunition is a close follow-up to the best of these).

Most 69-grain (or larger) bullets will not be stabilized enough for good accuracy if fired from twists of less than 1-in-10, the exception to this rule being the Speer's 70-grain SSP (semi-spitzer soft-point). It is designed for use in the 1-in-12 twist thanks to the bullet's less tapered shape, which allows it to be stabilized. The trade off with this 70-grain bullet is a decrease in ballistic coefficient, whereby it loses velocity faster over extreme distances. The power of this soft-point, though (especially for police sniper work) would make it capable of quicker stopping power than might be realized with lighter .223 bullets.

On the flip side of things, the .308 offers more power if the weapon must be used against lightly armored vehicles or the like. While the new 5.56mm SS109 ammunition comes close to rivaling much of the .308's performance, new SLAP rounds (see below) promise to leap-frog the .308 ahead in this area. With expanding bullets (which are an option to most police snipers), the wounds created by the .308 are massive enough to generally guarantee that a foe will be instantly dropped even with less-than-perfect bullet placement. While the .308 doesn't give much extra range over the new 5.56mm SS109 bullet, the .308 still bucks crosswinds a bit better, which can be an important consideration in many areas. Currently, the 150- and 180-grain Spitzer boat-tail rounds seem to be most ideal for sniper use, though this may vary according to the ammunition and firearm.

It must be remembered that a price is paid for the .308's pluses in the form of increased weight of both ammunition and rifle, as well as recoil that makes multiple or follow-up shots slower to carry out. When choosing a sniper chambering, careful thought must be given as to whether the .223 or .308 will better serve the task at hand.

Occasionally the .30-06 will also show up on police sniper teams. While many consider this to be an outmoded, antiquated round, anything the .308 can do, the .30-06 can do a bit better. The problem with using this round is the lack of modern rifles chambered for it which are suitable for sniping use. If a bolt-action rifle is to be used, however, the .30-06 is an option which may appeal to some snipers.

The Glaser Safety Slug is also available for the .308 and .30-06 (as well as a number of pistol rounds, including the 9mm Luger). The safety slug uses a copper jacket which surrounds a core of small, lead-shot pellets rather than a solid lead core. When the bullet hits a foe, it opens up shortly after penetrating the skin; the shot spreads out and cuts a large swath through the recipient's tissues. Such damage is very extensive and almost guarantees your victim will stop in his tracks instantly. While this in itself doesn't offer much over standard expanding bullets, the real plus comes if the sniper misses a shot: the safety slug tends to break apart and quickly lose energy rather than ricochetting dangerously to injure innocent bystanders (hence the name "Safety Slug").

On the negative side is the high cost of the Glaser Safety Slug as well as the fact that it is not quite as accurate as many other more conventional rounds. Glaser Safety Slugs are available from Phoenix Systems, Inc., for about $15.70 per pack of 6 rounds in 9mm Luger or about $23.60 or so for a pack of 6 rounds in either .308 or .30-06.

There are a number of arms chambered for the Russian 7.62x39mm round (especially those exported from communist countries and the Valmet line from Finland). While the 7.62x39mm packs a bit more punch than the .223/5.56mm, its lower speed gives it a trajectory that is not flat enough to be practical for many sniper applications. Unless the maximum range is only 200 yards, the sniper will have problems with bullet drop when making long-range shots with a 7.62x39mm rifle.

Currently, most of the major U.S. companies in the ammo industry don't offer the 7.62x39mm cartridge for sale, but this will probably change in the near future as more and more rifles chambered for this round become available to American shooters. Hansen Cartridge Company is importing noncorrosive Yugoslavian 7.62x39mm ammunition topped with 125-grain Spitzer bullets which would be suitable for sniper use. Avoid "bargain basement" 7.62x39mm ammunition imported from China or other countries which use corrosive primers; this ammunition demands careful cleaning after use even in guns with chromed barrels, and it generally isn't too accurate. (Tip: for those who reload this round, try to use lighter bullets so that the velocity of the bullet is increased and the trajectory flattened out a bit.)

For those who are forced to use FMJ bullets because of the conventions of war, it is possible to alter the tip of an issued bullet so that it will expand. This can be done by simply carving off the very tip of the bullet so that the lead just starts to show. Such alteration does not hurt accuracy but does make the bullet "illegal." While this practice seems to have been carried out since World War I by various troops throughout the world, each sniper should decide whether *he* really wants to break the rules, and whether the risks of being caught by an enemy with such rounds is worth the risk.

Care must be taken not to take off too much of the tip of an FMJ when expanding it in this way, since most FMJ bullets don't really have a full metal jacket: the copper coat ends at the base of the bullet exposing the bottom of the lead core. If too much of the tip of the jacket is removed, the core of the bullet may shoot through the jacket, leaving it behind in the rifle's bore. Such an obstruction can ruin the barrel of the rifle or even cause harm to the gun's receiver—as well as the shooter. (Currently, Speer is working on real full-metal jacketed bullets by plating a heavy copper coat right over the lead core so that the final jacket completely surrounds the core. This practice, however, is not yet widespread in the ammunition industry.)

In semiauto sniper rifles, cycling problems can be caused by too weak or too "hot" a load. A load that is too weak will cause the weapon to fail to either chamber a new round, cock the hammer, or—rarely—extract the cartridge (bear in mind the fact that all of these can be caused by failure of the firearm). Hot loads often cause the brass to stick to the chamber wall so that the bolt can't cycle back easily resulting in a broken extractor or a rim being torn off the brass, depending on the strength of the extractor. These problems can generally be avoided by using commercial ammunition or staying away from the limits listed in tables when reloading.

If a sniper uses expanding bullets, he should be sure cartridges will reliably chamber in his rifle. Damage done to the tip of a bullet during chambering will not hurt the accuracy of the round (damage to the base of a bullet will, for those who reload). Good crimps and cannelures on the bullets will help prevent a lot of feed failures and minimize damage to the cartridge. Cannelures also prevent bullets from cramming back into the brass during chambering (with resulting excessive pressures) and can help to promote bullet breakup upon entering a human target, in the case of fast twists with the .223 rifles.

Armor-piercing rounds of the past weren't too effective since they were usually made of steel or brass, which caused the bullet to quickly lose its velocity over any great distance so that it was incapable of penetrating the target. New armor-piercing bullets with steel inserts are a different story, since the lead in the bullet allows it to maintain its energy while the point ensures the penetration of armor. These rounds, considerably more effective when hitting human targets, are rather unstable, so they upset easily and thereby cause more damage. This is especially true of the new SS109 fired from a 1-in-7 twist.

One special rimfire load is the .22 CB Long Cap, which is offered by CCI and Federal Cartridge Company. The .22 CB Long Cap has the case of a .22 LR, but the bullet is lighter and the powder charge is quite a bit smaller. When fired from a .22 rifle, the shot is nearly silent, while having much greater weight and velocity than an air rifle pellet. This makes it ideal for use in "putting out" lights which may make nighttime movements of an assault group impractical.

While short barrels (like those of a pistol) don't cover up the sound of the CB Long, the barrel of most .223 rifles is long enough to muffle the sound; with a .22/.223 adapter cartridge like that offered by Harry Owen, it's possible to fire the CB Long from the centerfire rifle (in a manual cycling mode).

If forced to use the .22 for self-defense, your best bets are probably the high-speed CCI "Stinger," which creates a lot of damage to flesh-and-blood targets at ranges within fifty yards, with Federal HP

"Spitfires" and Winchester's "SuperMax" both doing nearly as well. For longer ranges, CCI's Mini-Mag LR HS, Federal's "Hi-Powers," or Winchester's 37-grain HP are good bets; Winchester's Silhouette ammunition (with a 42-grain lead bullet) is good for shooting at extreme .22 LR ranges (out to 100 or even 125 yards). For those needing extra accuracy, Winchester's R1 "Match" or Federal's Champion Target ammunition work well in most .22 rifles.

Integral silencers built around .22 rifles may sometimes be appropriate for some sniper use. Good silencers with standard-velocity .22 LR ammunition have very low noise signatures, which can be covered up by the background noise in many areas. Care must be taken to avoid the "hyper" .22 ammunition with silenced weapons, since the bullet will make a sonic crack once it leaves the barrel and breaks the sound barrier.

As mentioned earlier, centerfire rifles (as well as carbines chambered for the 9mm Luger) with suppressors operate with a lot of racket due to the sonic crack of the bullet. Silencers do, however, change the sound envelope enough so that many people mistake it for hammering or an engine noise of some sort. The location of the sniper is consequently much harder to find. Subsonic ammunition with heavier than normal bullets traveling below the speed of sound is also available for use with silencers; currently, the Olin Corporation's 9mm-OSM (Olin Super Match) is the round most suited for use in silenced sniper weapons, since it travels at subsonic speeds while still maintaining its accuracy. The 9mm-OSM uses a 147-grain HP bullet and is capable of firing very small groups and produces minimal muzzle flash.

For those snipers using the new .50-caliber rifles, the Olin Corporation is also producing military rounds that, just a few years back, would have been considered "exotic" indeed. One is the previously mentioned SLAP round, which has a sharp tungsten penetrator encased in a plastic boot. After the bullet leaves the barrel, the plastic sleeve drops away and the penetrator travels on at a high speed capable of defeating the light armor on the Soviet BMP armored personnel carrier. (A SLAP tracer round is also being produced; differences in the ballistics of the SLAP and standard .50 BMG ammunition do not allow standard tracers to be used in the same belt of ammunition with SLAP rounds in a machine gun.)

Another exotic round in .50 BMG is the MP

(Multi-Purpose) round being produced by Olin under license from A/S Raufoss. The MP bullet features an incendiary explosive charge which is detonated shortly after impact, giving it time to penetrate light armor before igniting. This delayed ignition makes it especially effective against vehicles and light armor where the bullet penetrates to create maximum destruction and fire. The round is ideal for use against lightly armored trucks and personnel carriers as well as airplanes and helicopters. It therefore increases a sniper's ability to do damage to a large number of enemy vehicles.

This round is known as the "MP NM140" in Europe (where Raufoss manufactures it) and as the "API MK 211 mod 0" by the U.S. Navy. (The U.S. Army designation is unknown at this time.)

Among the more readily available .50 BMG rounds are the US M33 Ball (not noted for its accuracy in sniper rifles as compared to hand-loaded ammunition), the M17 tracer (also comparatively inaccurate), and several blank training rounds. One interesting .50-caliber round is the "Limited Range Trainer" round, which might be of use where the penetration of a normal .50-caliber bullet is too great (such as in urban areas or when used in SWAT operations).

Currently, Hansen Cartridge Company is offering .50 BMG ammunition reloaded to standard military specifications. This is ideal for many sniper applications, and the brass can be reloaded for those wanting to create extra-accurate sniper rounds.

Regardless of whether the .22 LR or the .50 BMG round is being used in the sniper rifle, good ammunition with bullets capable of quickly bringing down a foe or severely damaging equipment is a must for the sniper. Proper ammunition will make it possible for the sniper to make accurate shots with devastating results for his enemy.

One new development for those using the .308 Winchester and having access to military ammunition is the new SLAP (Saboted Light Armor Penetrator) developed by the Olin Corporation (Winchester). Originally created for the .50 BMG (Browning Machine Gun), .308 versions of the SLAP are slated to become available soon. While not ideal for living targets, these high-velocity tungsten bullets would be ideal for sniper/saboteur work in destroying equipment.

Most snipers would do well to avoid using tracer ammunition since it is usually less than accurate and can give away one's position as well. The only exception to this would be for military snipers who

find that they must also offer protection for themselves or who might encounter an enemy at close ranges. In such cases, a number of successive shots may be fired in short order. Having one or two tracers at the bottom of a magazine is a good reminder that you're almost out of ammunition. One good source of tracer ammunition is Phoenix Systems, Inc.; cost is about $9.95 for a pack of ten 9mm Luger rounds, or about $10.95 per pack of ten for .223, .308, or .30-06 rifle ammunition.

Bullets designed for use in varminting have thin metal jackets which allow the round to quickly come apart so that it expends its energy in a small animal. These aren't effective in combat, since they may cause only a superficial wound. They might even break apart once they strike small obstacles like grass or twigs; in fact, with fast twists like the new 1-in-7 for .223 rifles, the bullets often tear apart in the air before coming anywhere near the target.

Varminting bullets are often marketed as "SX" (Super eXplosive), but not all are. In general, very light bullets often are designed for varminting work; when in doubt, go to a bit heavier bullet or one designed for hunting rather than varminting. Current saboted rounds for the .30-06 and .308 fall into this category. As they are generally a bit less accurate than their standard bullet counterparts, they therefore are generally best avoided for sniper use.

Which manufacturers offer the best ammunition for sniper use? A lot depends on the firearm itself, but there are several companies whose ammunition seems to outperform others in the field. Federal's "Hi-Shok" ammunition is ideal for sniper use in all calibers (this is certainly true in both the .308 and .30-06, as well as other centerfire chamberings used in some bolt-action sniper rifles). The soft-point Hi-Shoks are available topped with both 150- and 180-grain bullets in .308 and .30-06 ammunition. In .223, Federal offers ammunition with 55-grain bullets in soft-point, FMJ boat-tail, or HP (hollow point) boat-tail configurations.

Winchester also offers excellent "Silvertip" ammunition with the same 150- and 180-grain bullet weights for both the .30-caliber chamberings. With the .223, Winchester offers an excellent 53-grain HP as well as several 55-grain loads (including the low-priced bulk offerings mentioned above). Also notable for accuracy in nearly all of their chamberings is Norma ammunition, which is currently being distributed in the U.S. by the Federal Cartridge Company.

Most sniper rifles work very well with any of these rounds from both Winchester and Federal. Generally, a sniper should purchase a wide variety of ammunition for his rifle and test it out to see which cartridge performs best for him.

For those using carbines chambered for the 9mm Luger as sniper weapons, there is also a huge selection of ammunition available. In general, the Winchester Silvertips, Federal HP and "Nyclad," and CCI's "Lawman" JHP and "Blazer" JHP ammunition are the top choices among the many offered in the industry. In addition to being accurate, all of these rounds open up with great consistency so that the bullets quickly stop an opponent.

The 10mm (.40 caliber) pistol ammunition first proposed by Jeff Cooper is currently being offered by Norma (it will probably be manufactured by other companies as pistols chambered for the round become available). The 10mm would seem to be even more ideal for the sniper uses now filled by the 9mm Luger. The round has several hundred feet per second higher velocity and about twice the muzzle energy of the 9mm Luger while keeping a relatively flat trajectory. The down side to this type of ammo at the time of this writing is that no accurate carbines are currently available for it. Chances are this will change in the near future, in which case the new round will be worthy of consideration for limited sniper use.

Even more limited in capability than centerfire pistol rounds is the lowly .22 LR. While the .22 LR just doesn't have the energy needed for sniping (except, perhaps, for military harassment), there are a few uses to which it might be put by a police sniper.

3
Single-Shot Rifles

Back in the 1700s and 1800s, single-shot rifles were the "high-tech" of the day. Not so anymore, of course. Generally, snipers prefer having the quick second or third shot offered by a bolt or semiautomatic action.

The single-shot rifle does, however, enjoy a very strong lock-up, is lightweight (especially when compared to the anchor-like weights of many military sniper rifles), and often has great inherent strength—attributes often missing in other types of rifles suitable for sniper use. Therefore, some snipers looking at various types of rifles may choose the single-shot for their own use.

There are a number of modern reproduction firearms which are modeled after antique rifles. None of these are really suitable for sniper use, since accuracy is often less than precise and such firearms are often chambered for antique rounds whose rainbow-like trajectory makes precise bullet placement at various ranges much more difficult than with more modern rounds.

Two modern single-shot firearms are available, however, which have the accuracy needed for sniper use and which are chambered for modern rounds suitable for sniper use. These are the Ruger Number 1 rifle and the Thompson/Center Contender Pistol (which is also available in a rifle configuration).

Sturm, Ruger Number 1

The Sturm, Ruger Number 1 rifle is available in a number of configurations and is noted for its accuracy. Like other Ruger guns, the Number 1 is known for its strength and reliability; parts breakage is rare. With care, the Number 1 will function without needing maintenance other than careful cleaning and lubrication.

One model suited to sniper work is the No. 1B Single Shot. It is available in a number of chamberings, including .223, .257 Roberts, and .30-06, as well as several magnum chamberings (including the .338 Winchester Magnum).

The No. 1B comes with one-inch scope mounts and has integral mounts in its receiver. Like other Number 1s, it has a hammerless falling block design and an auto ejector, making reloading quick and simple. A tang safety is mounted at the upper rear of the receiver, where it is operated by the thumb. The stock and foregrip are made of walnut. For those wanting iron sights to back up the rifle's scope, the No. 1A Light Sporter and No. 1S Medium Sporter are viable alternatives. They are nearly identical to the 1B except for adjustable leaf sights and quarter ribs over the barrel.

The No. 1V Special Varminter has the greatest potential accuracy of all the variations of the No. 1, although it may be a bit heavy for some shooters. The No. 1V has a 24-inch heavy barrel and a semi-beavertail foregrip; the barrel is tapped for a target scope block with one-inch rings supplied by Ruger. The No. 1V comes in a number of chamberings,

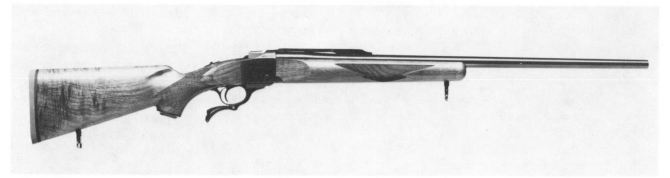

Single-shot rifles, like this Ruger No. 1B, have a strong lock-up and are lightweight compared to many other sniper rifles. Photo courtesy of Sturm, Ruger & Company.

A number of versions of the Ruger No. 1 are available. Shown is the Light Sporter 1A. Photo courtesy of Sturm, Ruger & Company.

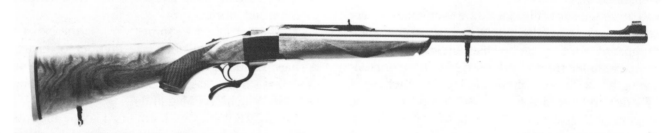

The No. 1S Medium Sporter is shown with folding rear sight and scope mount over the rear receiver/barrel. Photo courtesy of Sturm, Ruger & Company.

The Ruger Tropical Rifle is a handy single-shot similar to other Ruger No. 1 rifles. Photo courtesy of Sturm, Ruger & Company.

including the .223, .22-250, and .25-06.

The Ruger Number 1 is known for its accuracy and is a good choice as a single-shot sniper rifle.

Thompson/Center Contender
Pistol and Carbine

The quite accurate Thompson/Center Contender pistols are very versatile thanks to their quick-change barrels, which make changing to another ammo size quite simple. One frame can be used with any number of barrels of different lengths and chambers. There are several models of the T/C Contender pistol; most effective for "sniper pistol" use is the Super 14, with its 14-inch barrel and rubber-and-wood pistol grip.

The Super 14 comes with adjustable iron sights. Scope mounts are available from the factory, and many shooters are able to achieve rifle-like accuracy with the scoped pistols.

While such use might be ideal in very few sniper situations, more practical for sniper use is the company's new carbine based on the pistol action, but with a longer barrel and rifle-style stock. The carbine is currently offered with a semi-pistol grip stock and a 21-inch barrel which is drilled and tapped for easy scope mounting. The best calibers for sniper use are the .223 Remington, .357 Remington Maximum, and the .44 Magnum (the last two being powerful cartridges originally designed for revolvers but suitable for limited-range sniper use). Shooters who reload may also be interested in the 7mm TCU chambering.

Many of the under-16-inch pistol barrels fit on the carbine, and the carbine stock itself will fit on the T/C Contender pistol. Be sure to get a special permit if needed, since mounting the carbine stock on a pistol with a barrel of less than 16 inches in length or placing a short pistol barrel on the carbine may violate some state and federal legal length limits.

Choate Machine and Tool offers flash-hider extensions which can be welded onto 14-inch barrels to bring them to the 16-inch limit. Their cost is about $20, making the hiders a useful alternative for those who want a short barrel.

Choate also offers two styles of pistol grip stocks for the rifle. One stock is made of tough Zytel plastic, making the stock more impervious to humidity or wet weather than the standard stocks. The second features a steel folding stock with a Zytel pistol grip, making it possible to store a Contender in a very small space while still having it ready to use in a hurry. Cost for the standard stock is about $45, while the folder costs $68 or so. Choate also markets a plastic fore grip (which is presently selling for $12) which matches the two stocks described above. The Choate stock has a sling swivel attached to it which makes putting the carbine on a sling very practical (thanks to swivels on Choate's pistol grip as well as the stock itself).

Those who wish to use the pistol configuration of the T/C Contender will find Uncle Mike's large holsters for scoped Contender pistols ideal for carrying the gun about comfortably.

Specifications for Single-Shot Rifles

Name	Length (in.)	Weight Unloaded (lbs.)	Barrel Length (in.)
Ruger No. 1A Light Sporter	39.38	7.25	22
Ruger No. 1B Single Shot	43.38	8	26
Ruger No. 1S Medium Sporter	39-43	7.5-8	22-26
Ruger No. IV Special Varminter	41.38	9	24
T/C Contender (Pistol)	17.25	2.81	14
T/C Contender (Carbine)	35	5.13	21

4

Bolt-Action Rifles

Until recently, when semiauto military rifles became quite accurate, the bolt-action was *the* action for achieving the accuracy a sniper needed. Born in the early 1900s, the military bolt-action rifle on which most sniper rifles are based offers some real advantages. Because the action is simple, it is easy to maintain and repair, often making it a bit more reliable than many other rifle types. Because the bolt is manually operated, the rifle can also be used with a wider range of ammunition; rounds which fail to consistently cycle a semiauto will not create problems in a bolt-action rifle. Finally, because the stock and fore grip of the bolt-action rifle are generally made of one piece of wood or plastic, using the sling to steady the rifle won't cause the point of impact to wander about (which is often the case with semiauto military rifles). A bipod can be placed at the front of the stock without requiring that the rifle be rezeroed.

Innate accuracy aside, the bolt-action, when compared to the modern semiauto rifle, is not without its drawbacks. It doesn't dampen the recoil of the gun the way a semiauto action does, it's slower than a semiauto in making a follow-up shot or engaging a second target, and it doesn't allow a shooter to fire a second shot without a lot of movement.

The militaries and law-enforcement agencies of the world go around and around about whether the bolt-action or semiauto is more suited to sniper use. (Two good examples this are the current "throwbacks" to the bolt-action by the U.S. Marines and U.S. Army and the switch by the Germand Bundeswehr from their Heckler & Koch G3 rifle to a bolt-action Mauser for sniper use.) In fact, both actions can come very close to perfection, and sniper rifles based on either type offer accuracy undreamed of a few years back.

Just what determines the accuracy of a bolt-action? This is often a bit of a mystery, with the "fine tuning" of a sniper rifle being more of an art than a science.

One problem which disturbs the accuracy of any rifle is barrel whip, which is created when the bullet travels down a barrel once the gun is fired. The bullet's travel causes the barrel to vibrate and whip as the bullet leaves the muzzle, making its direction a bit off the center of aim. If the whip were consistent from one shot to the next, this wouldn't be a problem, but bullet whip varies from one shot to the next as the barrel heats up. The solution to the problem is a heavy barrel which dampens the amount of whip; it is for this reason that a heavy barrel is generally found on most sniper rifles. A fluted barrel is used when weight is more of a consideration than cost (with new computer-driven machinery, it is probable that the fluted barrel will become more common on sniper rifles in the near future).

The second reason for the heavy barrel has to do with heat build-up. A tremendous amount of heat is generated when a rifle is fired, a lot of which is absorbed by the barrel. Being made of metal, barrels expand as they heat up, and expansion occurs in all directions—forward, backward, and around the barrel's circumference. As it causes the barrel to push against the stock, this expansion can change the direction in which the barrel is aimed and cause bullet impact to shift with heat build-up, often resulting in a stringing in bullet pattern. While this isn't a problem if only one shot is fired, it is of concern when a group of shots is fired or when the gun is being zeroed.

One partial solution to this problem is to use a heavy barrel that will absorb the heat. This works for a time, but heat build-up still overcomes the insulating effects of a heavy barrel with just a few shots, so other measures are called for as well.

Doing away with the barrel taper is another partial solution. Doing so keeps the barrel from levering itself up out of the stock as it pushes forward during heat expansion. For this to work well, the stock must be very smoothly fitted to the barrel and the barrel without taper. Glass bedding (putting fiberglass or other material between the stock and the barrel) is most often the solution to getting this smooth fit.

Another way to achieve this is to free-float the barrel. Generally, this means having the action and the first few inches of the chamber end of the barrel supported by the stock, with the barrel a fraction of an inch away from the stock from there on out. One other variation of free-floating the barrel is to have the receiver/chamber area of the muzzle supported and then free-float the barrel from the action out to a pressure point placed under the tip of the fore end of the stock.

Since the barrel exerts pressure against the action along with the recoil of shots fired, the action itself must be snugly seated to the stock or it will shift from one shot to another. While, in theory, this shouldn't affect the zero of a rifle since the scope is mounted on the action (which, in turn, is fastened to the barrel), it often does hurt accuracy. To overcome this problem, the recoil lug must be bedded tightly to the stock, and the rear of the action must fit perfectly to the stock. Again, glass-bedding of the action is the most common way to achieve this (though some rifles, like the Ruger 77, achieve it by placing the screws fastening the stock to the action in such a way that a very tight fit is achieved without glass-bedding).

Finally, accuracy can be enhanced or hindered by the ammunition used in the rifle. With bolt-action rifles, the main problem seems to come in the bullet jump made across the gap in the chamber just before the rifling. This problem is often exacerbated in European rifles which have traditionally had a larger gap than American guns. (This is why European guns often give better accuracy with European ammunition, since the bullets are seated a bit farther out than U.S. ammunition in the same chambering.)

A good way to avoid this is to use a standardized round/chambering—which is one reason why many sniper rifles are now chambered for the .308 Winchester/7.62 NATO. The round has been more or less standardized by the West.

Because the "cherry" used to ream out the barrel to form the chamber of rifle barrels gradually wears out, there is always a slight variation in chamber size even from one rifle to the next from the same manufacturer.

These differences mean that a sniper must often experiment with various types of ammunition to achieve the highest possible accuracy, with some rifles all but demanding hand loads tailored to their peculiarities.

Bolt-action hunting rifles abound these days. Some of these sporters—especially those designed for varminting use—can, and often are, easily pressed into service as sniper rifles. The big plus of these rifles is their price; while most of the military/police sniper rifles carry price tags ranging from $2,000 to over $4,000 each, many quality varmint rifles cost only a few hundred dollars and have equally good accuracy. While purchasing a sniper rifle with a scope saves a lot of work for those needing a sniper rifle, those willing to do some shopping around to put a suitable scope and rifle package together can enjoy big savings.

Beretta 500/501/502

Beretta has a line of sporter rifles which are capable of giving the accuracy needed in a sniper rifle (especially if the purchaser takes time to bed or float the barrel). While no heavy-barrel version of the rifle is available, this rifle is ideal for those looking for a lightweight centerfire sniper rifle.

The Beretta 500/501/502 series has three receiver lengths to accommodate the various shell lengths that the guns are chambered for. The 500 rifle has short bolt throws and is chambered in .222 and .223; the 501, a medium length throw for .243 and .308; and the 502, the longest throw to accommodate the .270, 7mm Remington Magnum, .300 Winchester Magnum, .30-06, and .375 HH Magnum.

The receivers on all the rifles are drilled for a scope; no iron sights are supplied with the firearms (although they are available as options). Beretta also offers scopes which can be purchased with their rifles; these include the Hakko Mark VIII (3-9x40) and Zeiss Diavari ZA (1.5-6x 42). The high stock of the rifles makes it easy for most shooters to get a proper cheek weld when using a scope. The stock itself is made of walnut with a non-glare oil finish, and checkering is featured on the grip and fore grip. The metal on the rifles is blued and all models come with a black rubber recoil pad. The bolt handle curves down and is easy to grasp. The safety is located at the top of the receiver, just behind the bolt handle.

In addition to the quality work and design for which Beretta guns are known, the Beretta 500/501/502 series of rifles offers the sniper the wide range of chamberings mentioned above, which aren't available with many other bolt-action sniper rifles.

CETME Fusil de Precisión

The Spanish CETME (Centro de Estudios Técnicos de Materiales Especiales) Fusil de Precisión is fashioned after the country's old Mauser receiver with a heavy barrel and a Monte Carlo sporter-style stock. The rifle has iron target sights as well as a scope, with a tall, folding bipod available. The rifle is chambered for the 7.62 NATO round adopted by Spain in 1957 for its Model 58 assault rifle.

Daisy 601/602

These two Daisy sniper rifles appear to be based on the old Iver Johnson Models 300 and 400. The Daisy rifles have been greatly modified, however, and have a conventionally shaped, compositional stock with an adjustable pull length and Harris bipod under the foregrip. The rifles use a rotary box magazine (similar to that of Ruger's 10/22 rifle) and have a fluted barrel. The Model 601 is chambered for the .308/7.62 NATO and the Model 602 for the .416/.338 (858x71mm) wildcat cartridge.

Enfield L42A1

The Enfield rifle is a converted .303 No. 4 Mark I Enfield rifle rechambered for .308 Winchester with the stock modified to accept a cheek rest and shortened to "sporter" length. The rifle was normally deployed with the L1 Straight Sight Telescope by the British military. The police version

of the rifle, the Police Enforcer, usually had a 4- to 10-x power variable Pecar scope. Both rifles usually had iron sights as well. The L42A1 has very few features not found with other rifles and is generally considered as a second choice to many of the rifles described in this chapter.

FN Modele 30-11

The Fabrique Nationale 30-11 was created by modifying the company's big game rifle. The action itself is based on the Mauser design, and the rifle has the usual heavy barrel found on most of today's bolt-action sniper rifles; unlike many other bolt-action rifles, the FN 30-11 has a flash suppressor. The receiver sports a dovetail mount with a wide range of sighting devices available, including Anschutz iron sights and night-vision scopes. (Many of these sighting devices are mounted high, which is practical with the rifle's adjustable cheek rest. This places the barrel lower in relationship to the recoil so that recoil is straight back, enabling the sniper to watch the target more easily during recoil.)

The FN 30-11 rifle has a distinctive bolt handle that is curved back for easier use. The butt stock is made of two parts so that it can be quickly adjusted for length of pull by substituting longer or shorter sections; fine adjustments can be made with pad inserts. The cheek rest is also adjustable by the use of inserts. Currently, the rifle is available only in the .308 Winchester chambering.

Field Arms Mark 1 and Mark 5

Field Arms in London, England, is currently trying to carve out a niche in the military sniper rifle market. Its sniper rifles are fashioned after Sako hunting rifle actions and often incorporate Oy Vaimentninn Metalli Ab (of Finland) silencers into their design. Field Arms offers three models of bolt-action sniper rifles: the Mark (often abbreviated Mk) 1, Mark 3, and Mark 5.

The Mark 1 (which is very similar to the Vaime Mark 2 listed below) has an integral silencer and is chambered for the .308 Winchester. It can be used with either standard ammunition or special rounds loaded with heavy bullets (of around 277 grains) which travel at subsonic speeds to minimize rifle crack and muzzle noise. The Mark 5 is nearly identical to the Mark 1, but it has a fluted barrel with a muzzle brake/flash suppressor rather than a silencer.

Unfortunately, subsonic rounds are rather

inaccurate in the Mark 1 (as well as many other similar rifles), so that groups are generally in the range of two inches at one hundred yards—far from the accuracy provided by standard ammunition. Nevertheless, users of the Mark 1 will generally find this a good trade-off in exchange for the rifle's relatively quiet (though not silent) shooting.

The Mark 1 and Mark 5 wooden stocks have an adjustable cheek piece and a semi-pistol grip. Finishes include epoxy and crinkle paint in a variety of colors. The Mark 1 also has a buffer in its bolt to minimize noise made when cycling the action.

Fusil Model 1-A

The French are currently using the Fusil Model 1 as their military sniper rifle. Type "A" is the military sniper rifle, the "B" is the target rifle, and "C" sells to the hunting market. Length of pull is adjusted with butt-pad inserts, and a cheek pad is placed on the stock for use with telescopic sights (with iron sights being available as well). The 1-A has a bipod which folds up alongside its stock when not in use and has a pistol grip "tacked on" to its wooden stock. The barrel has a flash hider, and the magazine is of the detachable box style; the trigger pull is adjustable on these rifles. The 1-A rifle is available only in .308 Winchester.

Grendel SRT Sniper Rifle

The Grendel SRT was created as a sniper rifle which could be carried as easily and as light as a .223 assault rifle. To achieve this end, the SRT's design incorporates some unique features, including an injection molded Zytel plastic stock (with a rubber butt pad) which folds under the action of the magazine and partially nestles into the fore grip and around the magazine for a compact length of only thirty inches. In an effort to keep the weight of the rifle down without sacrificing accuracy, a free-floating fluted barrel is used on the SRT, and a muzzle brake is attached to keep the light rifle's

recoil at manageable limits. (The company literature states that the rifle is designed for use with a silencer; toward this end, the muzzle brake can be unscrewed and replaced by a silencer, while the rifling is designed for use with heavy, subsonic bullets.)

The rifle has a SAKO action with the safety located to the right of the receiver behind the bolt. A small extension to the front of the stock is designed for use with an M16 "clothespin" bipod. The forward part of the stock and fore grip are created from two injection moldings, which also form the rifle's magazine and trigger guard. The dovetail scope mounts on the SRT receiver are designed to accept standard one-inch scope rings or special clip-on emergency sights offered by Grendel.

Grendel currently offers a number of different rifle models with barrel lengths of 16, 20, and 24 inches and chamberings which include .22-250, .243, .308, and .358.

The Grendel SRT, with its plastic stock and light, fluted barrel, may very well be the shape of things to come.

Iver Johnson/RAI Model 300, Model 400

RAI (Research Armament Industries) originally designed three bolt-action sniper rifles in an effort to capture military sales. Since then, Iver Johnson has manufactured and marketed the "special-purpose" rifles. The Model 500, an upscale version of the rifle, is chambered for the .50 BMG cartridge while the smaller models, the Model 300 and Model 400, are chambered for .308 Winchester and a "wildcat" .338/.416 (8.58x71mm) cartridge, respectively.

Although not identical to the 500, the 300 and 400 rifles have the larger gun's "skeleton" look to them and are totally devoid of a fore grip. A tube projection (for the weapon's bipod) extends from the receiver under the fluted, free-floated, exposed barrel. A pistol grip is used in both rifles, and the

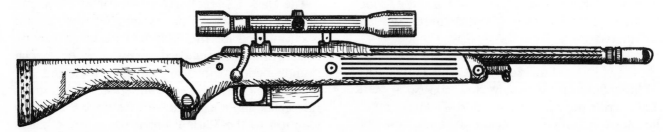

The Grendel SRT has an injection molded Zytel plastic stock (with a rubber pad), which folds under the action of the magazine. A free floating fluted barrel and a muzzle brake keep the rifle's recoil at manageable limits.

Kimber Model 84B Custom Classic chambered for .223 Remington. Photo courtesy of Kimber.

Close-up of Kimber Model 84 rifle showing safety, scope-mount blocks, bolt, and magazine release inside the trigger guard. Photo courtesy of Kimber.

stock is connected to its base and to the rear of the receiver. The butt of the stock is adjustable as is the cheek piece.

Models 300 and 400 were reputed to have very good accuracy but, since the Iver Johnson Company's bankruptcy and reorganization, it is presently unknown whether or not either model of the rifle will be manufactured.

Kimber Model 84

The U.S.-made Kimber rifles are sporters which might be adapted to sniper use. The Model 84 is a scaled-down, modified Mauser action designed specifically for the short .222/.223 family of cartridges. This makes for a lightweight rifle, even with a heavy varmint barrel. (One drawback to these rifles is the fact that they come with a highly polished finish. This is but a spray can of dull paint away for the sniper who is concerned about this. The rifle's beautiful hand-checkering and quality fitting work makes its price tag a bit higher than a "plain-Jane" model might demand.)

The ejection system departs from the Mauser design and uses a spring-loaded ejector reminiscent of the pre-1964 Winchester Model 70; both receiver and bolt are machined from bar stock. The adjustable trigger pull comes set at 2.5 pounds when it leaves the factory.

In addition to the .222 and .223 Remington, the rifles are also available in 6x47 (a wildcat based on the .222 Remington Magnum), 6x45 (the wildcat based on the .223 Remington), and true varminting rounds like the .17 Remington, .221 Remington Fireball and the .17 Mach IV (a wildcat created by necking down the .221 Remington Fireball).

Krico 640S/650S

The Krico company in Stuttgart, West Germany, has adapted its match rifle into a sniper configuration and is currently offering it in .222, .223, .243, and .308 chamberings. The finish of the sniper version has a matte-blue finish, an extra-large bolt handle, adjustable trigger pull weight, and a flash hider. The walnut stock has cooling slots cut into it and sports a spring-loaded, adjustable cheek pad with a vertically/horizontally adjustable butt pad.

The 640S safety is located to the right of the receiver, just behind the bolt slot. The bolt on many of these rifles is engine-turned, which makes an attractive, smooth-cycling action but also has a tendency to reflect sunlight. Some 640S users may wish to have this polish toned down somewhat.

Double-set triggers, night-vision mounts, or scopes (with 1.5-6x, 2.5-10x, or 3-12x variable powers) are available as options. Currently the Krico 640S is being imported into the U.S. by Beeman Precision Arms. A slightly modified version of the rifle, the 650S, is also seen from time to time; the two rifles are nearly identical, with the 650S being slightly heavier and longer.

Mauser SP66 and SR86

These sniper rifles are versions of the Mauser "66S Super Match" rifle designed for competition use. The SP66 is designed to fill the need by the police for a counter-sniper rifle while the SR86 is geared for military use.

The standard SP66 rifle, chambered for the .308 Winchester cartridge (with other chamberings available on special order), is fitted with a thumbhole, laminated wooden stock, which is fully adjustable for both length of pull and height of the cheek rest. The recoil pad is adjustable horizontally and vertically. The heavy barrel is equipped with a muzzle brake/flash hider and has optional iron

sights available; normally, though, only the Zeiss Diavari ZA 1.5-6x variable scope is used with it.

The trigger on the SR66 is adjustable from 1.5 to 2.2 pounds. Some snipers may find the use of a low-capacity, nondetachable magazine a drawback to this otherwise excellent rifle.

The SR86 is also normally chambered for the .308 Winchester. The main differences between this model and the SR66 are that the stock has a high cheek piece, a fluted barrel, cooling holes cut in the fore grip, no thumbhole/pistol grip, and a large capacity detachable box magazine. The Model SR86 normally is equipped with a 6x fixed scope, which is designed for sniper use. A bipod, iron sights, night-vision equipment, and a laser range finder are all available options for the SR86. Trigger pull is adjustable from 1.75 to 3 pounds.

Mossberg 1500

The Mossberg 1500 series of rifles is geared for the sporting market. However, in an effort to pick up police sales, the company offers a parkerized "Varmint Deluxe" version of its 1500. The walnut stock has a Monte Carlo style with a heavy rubber pad, and the rifle has an adjustable trigger pull. The safety is located at the upper right rear of the receiver, just behind the bolt handle. Chamberings available include .223 and .308; the nearly identical 1500 Varmint rifle with blued finish is also available in .223 or .22-250.

The 1500 rifles have a hinged floor plate in their integral magazine; a new 1550 series, nearly identical to the 1500 series, is also available with a detachable box magazine. While a heavy varmint barrel isn't currently available, it is likely that Mossberg will market such a rifle in the near future. If so, the 1550, with a heavy barrel, would also be ideal as a sniper rifle. Except for the different magazine layout, current production 1550s are nearly identical to the 1500 and are available in .243, .270, and .30-06.

Parker-Hale Model 82/83/85/87

These rifles are made by Parker-Hale Limited in Birmingham, England, and are based on the Mauser 98 action. The rifles use a heavy barrel epoxy bedded to a standard wooden stock, which is adjustable in length if you substitute extension butt pads on it.

The Model 82, adopted by both Australia and Canada (as the C3) for their military sniper rifles, has an integral magazine. The Model 83 has the magazine and feed way removed, allowing the barrel to be more tightly fitted to the action; this reduces the size of groups shot from the rifle to 1/2 MOA.

The newest variation of the rifle, Model 85, is aimed at the military market, while Model 87 is designed for police use. Both are available with synthetic or wooden stocks and bipods, and have larger capacity, detachable magazines; this latter feature is a great advantage. Model 85 has a large trigger guard (for use with gloves) and iron sights for emergency use, while Model 87 has a standard finger guard and uses only a scope for sighting. All models of the Parker-Hale sniper rifles are chambered for .308 Winchester.

Parker-Hale is also marketing the M87 Target Rifle for the sporting market, which is available with the parkerized finish found on other Parker-Hale models and has many of the features of the military versions (though the target rifle is available only with a wooden stock). The big plus is the wealth of chamberings for the M87 Target rifle. In addition to special calibers which can be ordered as an option, the rifle is sold in .308 Winchester, .243, 6.5x55mm, .30-06, and .300 Winchester Magnum. This "sporter" version of the Model 87 is currently imported into the U.S. by Precision Sports.

Remington Model 7

The Model 7 is the lightest of Remington's bolt-action rifles; much of the weight reduction is achieved by shortening the rifle barrel. The action is also shorter than usual, thereby limiting the chambering to shorter rounds, such as the .223, .243, 7mm-'08, 6mm, and .308. This short length also makes the rifle easier to use in tight quarters; one drawback is that shots will have a bit more muzzle blast and flash than those from guns with longer barrels.

Like most other Remington bolt-action rifles, the Model 7 has its safety lever on the top right of the receiver just to the rear of the bolt. The rifle comes with adjustable iron sights, and the receiver is drilled and tapped for easy scope mounting.

In addition to the standard wooden stock, an "FS" variation of the Model 7 is available with a fiberglass stock. Finishes with these stocks include gray and camouflage.

Remington "Sportsman" 78

The Remington 78 is relatively inexpensive when compared to other rifles in the Remington line (as well as those of other companies). The rifle has a hardwood stock devoid of checkering and the

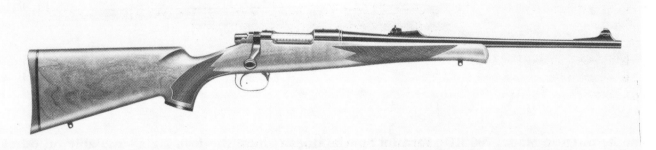

The Remington Model 7 is the lightest of Remington's bolt-action rifles due to the shortened barrel and action of the rifle. Photo courtesy of Remington Arms Company.

The Remington Model 7 FS has a tough fiberglass stock that is reinforced with Kevlar, making the rifle both lightweight and durable. Photo courtesy of Remington Arms Company.

metal doesn't have a high finish (which is a real plus for any sniper rifle). The rifle has iron sights, is drilled for scope mounts, and is available in .223, .243, .308, .270, or .30-06.

Many people who are interested in building a sniper rifle use the Remington 78 action for the basis of their gun and then add a heavy barrel and a custom stock. This does, of course, raise the price of an otherwise inexpensive rifle, but the quality of the action often makes such efforts worthwhile.

Remington 700/M24/M40

The 700 has long been one of the favorites of military and police sniper teams and enjoys popularity with many hunters as well. It is available in a number of models, including left-handed versions and heavy barrel varmint. During the Vietnam War, the U.S. Marines used the Remington 700 (designated the M40) in .308 as their sniper rifle.

For those looking for lighter weight, the 700 BDL is a good bet. It also has iron sights in addition to its drilled and tapped receiver. The 700 BDL is available in .223, .243, .270, .308, and .30-06.

Marketed by Remington specifically for the law-enforcement community, the Model 700 Police rifle has a heavy bull barrel which is drilled and tapped for a scope and is devoid of iron sights. The 700 Police has a parkerized finish, and the Monte Carlo-style stock has a low luster finish as well. The two chamberings available for it are the .223 and .308.

Remington also offers the lightweight Model 700 Custom KS Mountain Rifle, which has a tough Kevlar stock in both left- and right-handed versions. The stock is especially suited for use in wet conditions since it is highly resistant to moisture as well as abuse. To help absorb the recoil with the lighter rifle, a thin rubber recoil pad is used. Like most other 700s, the Mountain Rifle is designed for scope use and lacks iron sights. It is chambered for a wide range of cartridges, including .270 Winchester, .280 Remington, .30-06, 7mm Remington Magnum, .300 Winchester Magnum, and the .375 H&H Magnum. A similar model, the Model 700 RS comes with a glass-reinforced thermoplastic stock which is slightly less durable than the Kevlar stock; it is also several hundred dollars cheaper, thereby making it a practical alternative for those on a limited budget.

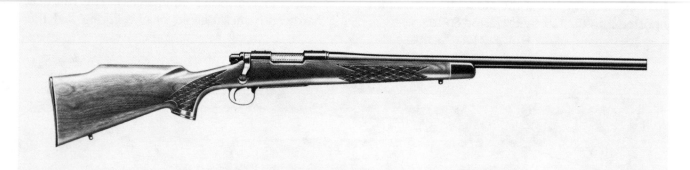

The Remington Model 700 BDL Varmint Special doesn't have the iron sights available on other BDL models, but its heavy bull barrel makes it ideal for many sniper applications. Photo courtesy of Remington Arms Company.

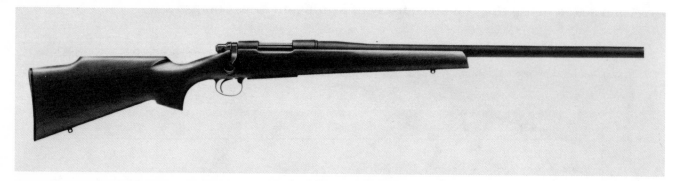

The Remington Model 700 Police is designed specifically for law enforcement use. The rifle has a heavy bull barrel which is drilled and tapped for a scope and devoid of iron sights. Metal parts are parkerized and the stock has a low luster finish. Photo courtesy of Remington Arms Company.

For anyone looking for the utmost in accuracy, the Model 40-XB Rangemaster target rifle, available in both single-shot and 4-round magazine versions, is a good bet. For most sniper work, the multi-shot version makes the most sense. It is available in .223 Remington, .308 Winchester, and 7mm Remington Magnum, while the single-shot version includes all these plus the .30-06. The action of the 40-XB is hand-bedded to the stock, and the heavy bull barrel is free-floated forward from the action. The trigger pull is externally adjustable. The 40-XBs are tested for accuracy at the factory and only shipped out if they are capable of shooting five-shot groups 1 MOA or less (the accuracy is guaranteed by Remington).

The M40, used by the U.S. Marines, was created in the early 1970s based upon lessons learned with the 700s used in Vietnam. The rifles were basically heavy-barreled Remington 700s with a dull finish and were nearly identical to the 40-XB. The M40 was slightly improved in the 1980s through the addition of a better barrel and a new scope system; this improved model is designated as the M40-A1.

The M40-A1 uses the action of the Remington 700 coupled with a camouflaged fiberglass stock and a heavy barrel chambered for the .308 Winchester/7.62 NATO. The barrel is a stainless-steel Atkinson heavy barrel, which is purchased by Marine armorers as a blank. It is then crowned and threaded by the armorer, who also beads the action and barrel to the stock. The bull barrel is free-floated in the stock to within one inch of the action. Once assembled, the rifle is test-fired and must be able to place five shots within 1 MOA before it can leave the armorer.

The M40 had a Leatherwood-modified Redfield 3-9x power variable scope with range-finding reference lines built into it to help the sniper compensate for bullet drop. The M40-A1 has a Unertl steel-tubed scope designed specifically for sniper use.

While little is currently known as of this writing about the U.S. Army's new M24 sniper rifle, it apparently will be based on the Remington 40-XB with a multi-shot magazine and chambered for .308, though some thought is being given to the use of a heavier round like the .300 Winchester Magnum.

The Remington Model 40-XB target rifle gives the utmost in accuracy and is available in both single-shot and 4-round magazine versions. Photo courtesy of Remington Arms Company.

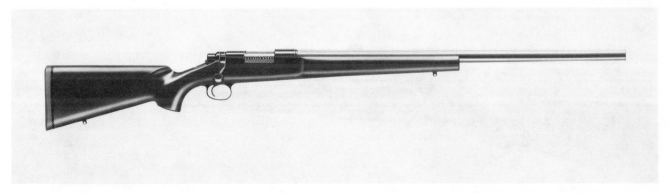

With a tough synthetic Kevlar stock, the Remington Model 40-XB Varmint Special target rifle gives high accuracy in the worst of environments. Like other 40-XB's, it is guaranteed to shoot five-shot groups of 1 MOA or less. Photo courtesy of Remington Arms Company.

Ruger 77

Ruger bolt-action rifles pack a lot of quality for their price thanks to the use of investment castings and good design characteristics. (Armchair authorities to the contrary, investment castings are actually stronger than parts milled from bar stock. The Ruger 77 action is the strongest available.) Most important to the sniper (in addition to their reasonable price), the 77 rifles are capable of excellent accuracy.

The 77s have a scope block molded into their receivers and come with scope rings designed to fit the receiver. This design does away with the need for screwing a scope mount block to the top of the receiver as well as the possibility of the mount working loose (as sometimes happens with other rifles). While this problem can be avoided with a scope mount, not having to bother with the problem at all is one advantage of the Ruger design.

A "live rubber" recoil pad is included with all 77s, which makes them considerably more comfortable to shoot even with the heavier recoiling cartridges. The trigger pull is adjustable (a gunsmith can also adjust the trigger overtravel if necessary), and the bolt action is one of the smoothest on the market. Many shooters also find the tang safety at the rear of the receiver easier to operate than many other safeties found on bolt-action rifles. Another plus is that the magazine floor plate can be released and the cartridges removed from the magazine without having to cycle them through the action; the release is located at the inside front of the trigger guard.

For cleaning, the bolt of the 77 is easily removed from the receiver without any tools. The Ruger rifle is also noted for its wide and strong extractor claw, which assures trouble-free performance. Some rifles have the bolt handle brazed or welded on, which can lead to problems with bolt handles occasionally coming off. The 77 doesn't have this problem, since its handle is part of the casting making up the bolt itself. In fact, the handle is strong enough to be used as a "safety lug," which locks into the receiver to hold the bolt in place should failure of the two locking lugs occur when using ammunition that creates dangerously high pressures.

As with many other rifles, the 77 comes in a wealth of models. Models with the "R" suffix have scope rings with them; "L" stands for Lightweight; "I" is for the International, with a full-length stock; and models with an "S" have iron sights. All told, there are five different models of the 77 with a choice of—at last count—some fifteen different chamberings between them, giving the sniper a wide choice of style and chamberings.

The rear sights on "S" models are of a flip-down design, which is adjustable for windage and elevation (by using a small screwdriver) and enables the sight to be flipped down when a scope is used. The front sight is excellent, having a gold bead which is readily visible in most types of lighting.

The 77RL Ultra Light is, as its name suggests,

Available in .243, .270, .22-250, .308, and .30-06, the weight of the 77RL Ultra Light is ideal for snipers who carry a rifle for long periods. Photo courtesy of Sturm, Ruger & Company.

Noted for its accuracy, the Ruger 77V Varmint rifle is one of the first choices for those wanting a bolt-action sniper rifle. With standard ring mounts, the 77V has a drilled and tapped barrel for target-scope blocks. Photo courtesy of Sturm, Ruger & Company.

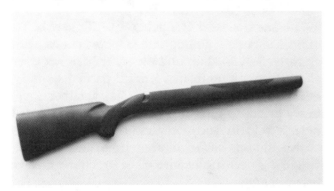

Glass-filled plastic stocks are offered by Ram-Line for many Ruger 77 rifles. The stocks are resistant to heat and moisture. Photo courtesy of Ram-Line.

very lightweight and ideal for snipers needing to carry a rifle for an extended period of time. It is available in a number of chamberings, including .243, .270, .22-250, .308, and .30-06.

The 77V Varmint rifle offers the greatest accuracy. It has standard ring mounts and a drilled and tapped barrel for target-scope blocks for those who wish to use larger scopes. Ruger offers a wide range of chamberings for the 77V, including .22-250, 6mm, .220 Swift, .243, .25-06, and .308 Winchester. Most 77V rifles are capable of shooting sub-MOA groups, given quality ammunition.

For increased durability in harsh environments, Ruger offers a laminated wooden stock (designated by a "Z" suffix for the zebralike pattern created). Ruger uses green and brown dyes in the different layers of wood to create a camouflage effect.

Glass-filled plastic stocks are also offered by Ram-Line for the 77 rifles. The black stocks are heat- and moisture-resistant and are 30 percent lighter than comparable wooden stocks. Available for the 77R, 77RS, and 77ST Ruger models, the Ram-Line stocks cost about $125.

Fast becoming a favorite of many police sniping teams, the Ruger 77 is an excellent choice for those wishing to have a high-quality rifle carrying a relatively low price tag.

SIG-Sauer SSG 2000

This bolt-action rifle, available in .308 Winchester, .300 Weatherby Magnum, .223 Remington, and 7.5mm Swiss, is another firearm which has come out of the collaboration between SIG (Schweizerische Industrie-Gesellschaft, or Swiss Industrial Company of Switzerland) and J. P. Sauer & Sohn (of Germany).

With a detachable box magazine and a flash suppressor/muzzle brake, the SSG 2000 has butt pad inserts to adjust length of pull. The rifle also has features not found on many other sniper rifles, including indicators to let you know the firing pin is cocked and whether or not a round is chambered, as well as a set trigger, a "mirage band" running down the top of the barrel (said to prevent heat mirage in the scope), and automatic decocking of the striker when the bolt is opened. Another interesting feature of the SSG 2000 is that its bore tapers slightly at the muzzle, causing the bullet to be swagged slightly and, in theory at least, making for a more accurate shot.

The action can be cycled quite quickly thanks to a reduction of the bolt handle lift to just 65 degrees (rather than the usually fuller stroke encountered in other bolt-action rifles). The bolt itself is fluted with its bearing edges (as well as the inside of the receiver) polished to reduce friction.

The adjustable-pull trigger can be worked in the conventional manner or used as a set trigger by pushing it forward. This readjusts the trigger pull so that it trips at slightly less than a pound. (If the shot is not fired, the trigger can be unset by raising the bolt handle.) Pulled hard to the rear when the bolt is open, the trigger also doubles as the bolt release.

The tang safety is one feature which some may dislike. While tang safeties are normally the easiest to use on conventional hunting rifle-style stocks, the SSG 2000's semi-pistol grip makes the tang safety a bit awkward to use.

The SSG 2000 is most often offered with the Zeiss Diatal-ZA 8x56mm T scope, which gives the user both high power and a rather wide field of view.

Springfield Armory Model 700 BASR

Currently, Springfield Armory (the commercial company, not the U.S. military armory which is now closed) offers a Model 700 sniper rifle based upon the Remington 700 action. The Springfield gun has a camouflaged fiberglass stock with a rubber recoil pad and a Douglas heavy barrel (with an optional stainless-steel barrel). The barrel is drilled and tapped for scope mounts and bedded in the stock. Chambered for the .308 Winchester, the rifle is guaranteed by Springfield Armory to fire MOA groups.

The 700 BASR comes with a choice of options, including a Leupold 3.5x10 variable scope with mounting hardware, night-vision scope mount, and rifle carrying case.

Sterling Sniper Rifle

The Sterling Armament Company of Dagenham, England, markets its rifle in .308 Winchester. As is the case with many other sniper firearms, the Sterling rifle is basically a sporter converted to military use. The heavy barrel is glass-bedded in a wooden, Monte Carlo stock, with optional bipod and night-vision equipment available.

Steyr SSG

The Austrian Steyr-Manlicher SSG rifles are being offered in target, hunting, and sniper versions, with all three fashioned around the same basic receiver and incorporating many identical parts. Like most other sniper rifles, the SSG69 has a rather long, heavy barrel to give bullets a greater than normal muzzle velocity and accuracy. The barrel also has a two-and-one-half-inch seating in the receiver, where it is heat-shrunk into place to achieve greater barrel rigidity.

Springfield Armory's 700 BASR sniper rifle has a camouflaged fiberglass stock with a rubber recoil pad and Douglas heavy barrel. Photo courtesy of Springfield Armory.

The SSG69 military sniper version has been adopted for use by Austrian military snipers. The rifle uses a green plastic (ABS "Cycolac") stock to minimize adverse effects caused by inclement weather. Two types of detachable magazines are available: a 5-round, metal rotary magazine with a rear face of clear plastic (which allows the user to determine how many rounds are left) and the 10-round staggered box magazine. The rotary magazine fits flush with the bottom of the receiver while the 10-round magazine extends from the bottom of the rifle.

The SSG69 is made in both .308 Winchester and .243 Winchester chamberings. A number of useful features are available, including a cocked striker indicator, removable spacers which allow the adjustment of length of pull from 12.5 to 15 inches, adjustable trigger pull (with optional double-set triggers available), and a nonglare finish. The rifle also has metal sights to back up the optical system consisting of a Kahles steel-tube ZF 69 6-power scope which compensates for bullet drop from 110 to 880 yards. The rifles are tested at the factory and adjusted to give minute-of-angle accuracy. The SSG69 was marketed in the U.S. as the SSG during the early 1980s.

In the mid-1980s, a slightly modified version of the rifle, the SSG-PII, was introduced. The principal differences between the SSG69 and SSG-PII are a modified bolt shape (taken from the target version of the SSG rifles) which is easier to grasp and a heavier barrel devoid of iron sights. A Litton M-845 night-vision scope is available as an option.

Vaime Mark 2

The Vaime Mark 2 appears to be very similar to the Field Arms rifles, though the model numbers seem to be different. Little is known about Vaime of Finland's "sniper systems" at the time of this writing, but it appears that the bolt-action .308 rifle is more or less typical of other rifles in its group except for the integral silencer built around the barrel. When subsonic ammunition is used in the Mark 2, sound levels are said to be about the same as that of a standard .22 rifle. The rifle is distributed in the U.S. by North American Sales International.

Winchester Model 70

The Model 70 has long been one of the rifles upon which military and police sniper rifles have been modeled. Model 70s were given what many consider an inferior redesigning during the mid-

Steyr SSG-PII has a barrel devoid of iron sights. Note the double set of triggers and butt inserts which allow the user to change the rifle's length of pull. Photo courtesy of Gunsouth.

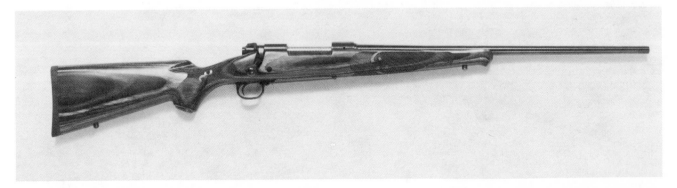

The Winchester Model 70 is shown with a Win-Cam camouflaged stock. This laminated stock has layers which are dyed in contrasting green and brown. Photo courtesy of U.S. Repeating Arms Company.

1960s, and the company had quality-control problems from 1964 through 1972 as well. Fortunately, Winchester has these problems cleared up so that post-1972 rifles have the same quality as the pre-1964 Model 70s—with a lower price tag.

The Winlite model has a Kevlar/graphite stock which makes the rifle nearly impervious to the elements; Ram-Line also offers an excellent plastic stock for about $125 which can be mounted on many 70 models (but, unfortunately, not on the varmint barrel model at the time of this writing).

The trigger pull and overtravel on the 70s can be adjusted by a gunsmith; this isn't a job for anyone else since it is a rather tricky operation. The Model 70s don't come with iron sights except for some of the XTR models or the no-frills Ranger models; this is generally not a consideration for those needing a sniper rifle, however. The three-position safety is located to the right of the receiver just behind the bolt handle.

The most ideal Model 70 for sniper use is the 70 XTR Sporter Varmint rifle, available in .22-250, .223 Remington, and .243.

The Winlite is one version of the Winchester Model 70 and has a Kevlar/graphite stock. Photo courtesy of U.S. Repeating Arms Company.

For those wanting iron sights to back up their scopes, the Winchester XTR Model 70 versions are ideal. Shown is the Sporter Magnum. Photo courtesy of U.S. Repeating Arms Company.

When weight is a consideration, the Featherweight XTR version of the Winchester Model 70 would make an ideal sniper rifle. Photo courtesy of U.S. Repeating Arms Company.

Perhaps the best of the Winchester Model 70s for sniper use is the 70 XTR Sporter Varmint rifle, which is available in .22-250, .223 Remington, and .243. Photo courtesy of U.S. Repeating Arms Company.

Specifications for Bolt-Action Rifles

Name	Barrel Length (in.)	Weight Unloaded (lbs.)	Length (in.)	Magazine Capacity
Beretta 500	24	6.8[1]	44	5
Beretta 501	23	7.5[1]	43	5
Beretta 502	24	8.4	44	4/5
CETME Fusil de Precisión	25.2	10.36	45.57	5
Daisy 601	24	13	42	5
Daisy 602	26	15.5	46	4
Enfield L42A1	27.5	10	46.5	5
FN 30-11	19.76	10.69	43.97	9
Field Arms Mk 1	26	9.2[1]	46	4
Field Arms Mk 3	20	7[1]	40	6
Field Arms Mk 5	26	9.9[1]	46	4
Fusil 1-A	21.7	11.43	44.7	10
Grendel SRT	20	6.6	40.8	9
Iver Johnson Model 300	?	?	?	5
Iver Johnson Model 400	?	?	?	4
Kimber Model 84	24	7.25	42.5	5
Krico 640S	26	9.6[1]	44.75	4
Krico 650S	26	10.6[1]	46	4
Mauser SP66	26.8	13.5	46	3
Mauser SR86	25.37	12.75	47	9
Mossberg 1500 Varmint	22	9.32[1]	44	5 or 6[2]
Parker-Hale M82	25.98	10.56	47.75	4
Parker-Hale M85/87	27.63	13.75	45.37	10
Parker-Hale M87 Target Rifle	26	10[1]	45	5
Remington 7	18.5	6.25[1]	37.5	4
Remington 78	22	7[1]	41.5	4
Remington 700 "Police"	24	9[1]	43.5	4
Remington 40-XB	27.25	11.25[1]	47	4
Ruger 77RL	20	6[1]	40	4
Ruger 77RS	22-24	7[1]	42-44	4
Ruger 77V	24-26	9[1]	44-46	4
Ruger 77/22	20	5.75[1]	39.75	10
SIG-Sauer SSG 2000	24	14.5	47.62	4
Springfield 700 BASR	26	11[1]	46	5
Sterling Sniper Rifle	26.5	9	44.4	4
Steyr SSG69	25.6	10.32	44.88	5 or 10
Steyr SSG-PII	26	10.69	44.5	5 or 10
U.S. Marines' M40	24	9.5	43.5	5
U.S. Marines' M40-A1	24	14	44	5
Winchester Model 70	20	6.25[1]	40.5	5
Winchester M. 70 XTR "Sporter Varmint"	24	7.75[1]	44	5

[1]Weights do not include scope since these rifles are often sold without scopes by the company marketing them.
[2]Capacity varies according to the chambering of the rifle.

5

Semiautomatic Rifles

Most semiauto sniper weapons are designed after modern military rifles and, as mentioned previously, many modern assault rifles have sufficient accuracy to be used as sniper rifles simply by adding a good scope and perhaps a cheek rest of some sort. Thus, it isn't uncommon to find a G3, SG510, FN LAR, AR-15, or even the old M1 Garand being used as a sniper rifle.

There are a number of advantages to using a sniper rifle that is similar—or even identical—to the issue military rifle.

For one thing, because military rifles are used under very adverse conditions, most designs have been debugged and perfected to the point where they are stronger and more reliable than most other rifle systems. They are designed for easy maintenance and repair and can operate under temperatures that adversely affect other rifles, including many bolt-action weapons.

Should the sniper be called upon to lay down suppressive fire, defend himself at close ranges, engage a large number of targets of opportunity, or be forced to fire upon a plane or similar large piece of equipment, a modern military semiauto rifle with a large-capacity magazine has many advantages not found in a bolt-action rifle.

Even when engaging a single target, the sniper has an edge when using a semiauto rifle, since the semiauto tames the rifle's recoil, making it possible to watch the target through the scope immediately following the shot to see if one's foe has been hit.

There is also a psychological advantage in using the semiauto in that the sniper knows that his rifle is ready for a second shot without having to manually cycle the weapon and possibly give away his position in the process. (During World War II, one of the more common complaints of British snipers was that they were often discovered when they cycled the bolt on their rifles for a follow-up shot.)

One potential problem with some of the rifles listed below is barrel flex. While rifles like the M14/M1A and Garand enjoy a one-piece stock and fore grip, more modern rifles like the FN LAR and AR-15 have their receivers supporting the barrel (rather than the stock supporting the barrel). This means that, in order to maintain accuracy, care must be taken to minimize the pressure placed against the barrel and fore grip. A sling attachment which pulls the barrel to one side or a bipod on the barrel itself can cause enough of a temporary barrel flex to shift the point of impact by several inches at one hundred yards.

Three solutions currently used to minimize barrel flex are to free float the barrel inside a fore grip which attaches to the receiver, or to use a heavy barrel; use a fluted barrel which keeps the rifle light while keeping the barrel rigid (which is already being done by SGW on its AR-15-style rifles); or, a solution which is seldom seen, to create a one-piece stock that surrounds the receiver and combines the fore grip to the butt stock. Use of bipods attached toward the rifle's receiver end rather than the muzzle end and holding the rifle with the off hand supporting the receiver under the magazine will also minimize barrel flex.

AR-10

The AR-10 was a weapon ahead of its time when it was developed in the early 1950s and—although the AR-15, modeled after the AR-10, enjoyed a huge commercial success—the AR-10 rifle never sold well. Experimental versions of the rifle were apparently originally chambered for the .30-06, while production and military rifles used in testing were in .308 Winchester (the then new 7.62mm NATO standard round). Sudan and Portugal adopted and purchased limited numbers of the rifles, but AR-10 sales weren't sufficient to keep any company in business, so the model was finally discontinued.

A number of other experimental versions of the AR-10 were also created by Colt Firearms (which had purchased the right to manufacture the rifle) in an effort to capture some part of the military small-arms market. The U.S. Army actually tested a Rock Island modified AR-10 as a sniper rifle candidate in 1977, but no large military force seemed overly interested in the AR-10.

The AR-10 has since become a collector's gun, with many owners building rifles around homemade receivers and other handmade parts, coupled with the few surplus parts still available. Many of these rifles have proven to be quite accurate, and the basic design would seem to lend itself to sniper use.

(One interesting demonstration of the potential accuracy of these rifles was given by Louis T. Cabrillo, Jr., an expert do-it-yourselfer, who assembled two AR10s using kits created from surplus Sudanese and Portuguese parts. He found

the rifles were able to achieve sub-MOA groups using the original barrels made for the weapons. Such groups suggest that the basic AR-10 would be quite capable when used as a sniper rifle.)

The Rock Island modification of the rifle consisted of free-floating the barrel inside a rigid fore grip attached to the receiver; it had the carrying handle/rear sight and front sights removed and a scope mount block placed on the upper receiver (in the manner currently used with the Insight Systems' sniper rifle modeled after the AR-15). The accuracy of this test rifle is unknown, but it probably was capable of firing at least 1 MOA groups and perhaps much better.

Although the AR-10 has been crowded out by the FN LAR, AR-15, M14, and other successful rifles, the basic design is still of merit. Now that the patent rights to the AR-10 have expired, several companies in the U.S. are toying with the idea of producing rifles based on the AR-10 (with one manufacturer working toward creating a rifle using plastic, rather than aluminum, receiver halves). Should these actually go into production, it would seem likely that the weapon could be easily modified into an excellent .308-caliber sniper rifle that would operate in the same manner as the AR-15 used by many military and police groups worldwide.

AR-15

When first introduced, the AR-15 was found to be dependable and deadly. Unfortunately, when the U.S. military adopted it, it made several changes in the design, used a powder that caused the rifle to cycle too fast and which clogged the gun's gas tube, and didn't issue cleaning kits or otherwise help troops maintain the weapon. Not surprisingly, the once-dependable rifle became a poor performer

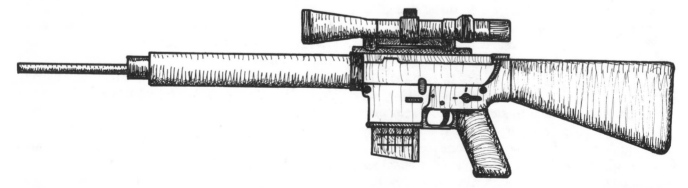

The AR-10 has the inherent accuracy of a good sniper rifle. In 1977, the U.S. Army tested a modified AR-10 as a sniper rifle candidate. The rifle had the carrying handle and front sight removed and the barrel floated inside the hand guard.

during the Vietnam War.

But the problems were finally rectified, and now the newest version of the rifle, the AR-15 A2 (or M16A2 in the military version) has proven to be reliable and accurate.

One example of its reliability arose in the 1980 NATO trials to select a standard 5.56mm round. During the tests, records were kept of the malfunctions of the various rifles used. The M16A1—the military's version of the AR-15—proved to be the most reliable weapon in the group (which included the Galil, FAMAS, Enfield IW, and FNC). Likewise, a gun writer who recently purchased an AR-15 A2 model of the rifle discovered that it didn't malfunction once during the test firing of several thousand rounds of ammunition; he had to quit the test when he ran out of cartridges!

The newest version of the rifle is as accurate as it is dependable. In fact, the U.S. Army has discovered that new M16A2 rifles are as accurate out of the box as highly reworked and modified M14 rifles, which were hand-built for the Army rifle teams who engaged in competition shooting. While the U.S. military specification for the new M16A2 requires that it shoot within 1.4 MOA, many of the new A2 models (both the civilian semiauto versions and the military rifles) are capable of shooting 1 MOA groups without any modification whatsoever.

A word about variations of the AR-15 is in order, since the wealth of designations can cause some confusion. The original model used by the U.S. Army and Air Force was the M16. Later, the Army added a forward assist to the rifle as well as other minor changes, and the new rifle was designated the M16A1. Other variations include a shortened carbine (the Commando, or XM177E2) usually chambered for .223 but also made in 9mm Luger as well as H-BAR (heavy barrel) weapons, the M231

Port Firing Weapon, SAW (Squad Automatic Weapon) models, and LMG (Light Machine Guns).

One advantage all these versions share is that a police or military team can equip itself with weapons which are all operated/controlled in an identical manner while being capable of filling different roles. Members of the AR-15 weapons family can fulfill the need for submachine guns, sniper rifles, assault rifles, or light machine guns. (The ability to conceal the presence of a sniper among other members of the group can have its finer points, especially for police teams. Many SWAT units have found that an AR-15-equipped sniper "blends in" with other members of the team who carry AR-15s so well that the sniper is "concealed" from the press after a hostage-taker has been "taken out;" this can help to avoid awkward questions, as well as keeping the sniper from being open to verbal attack.)

The M16A2 model was developed as a result of the 1980 NATO decision to switch to a heavier .223 bullet. Such a switch required a change to a 1-in-7 twist in order to stabilize the projectile. Since this was a major modification, the U.S. military decided to make a number of other changes as well. Included were a switch to finger-adjustable knobs for elevation and windage to the rear system; a new pistol grip; brass deflector; and a three-round burst mode rather than a full auto. (The Canadian military has adopted the M16A2 as its C7 rifle. Apparently, tank and APC [armored personnel carrier] crews will have the carbine version of the M16, to be designated the C8. Both weapons differ from the U.S. rifles in that they have the full-automatic setting rather than the three-round burst mode.)

The civilian version of the M16A1 (with the 1-in-12 twist) is the AR-15 Sporter; the M16A2 counterpart is the AR-15 A2 Government (Colt

The civilian version of M16A2, the AR-15 A2 Sporter II, has the forward assist of the M16A2 but not its finger-adjustable rear sights. Photo courtesy of Colt Industries.

The AR-15 A2 Sporter II H-BAR has finger-adjustable rear sights and all the features of the military H-BAR except for the burst mode. Photo courtesy of Colt Industries.

The Colt AR-15 A2 H-BAR (top) and Colt AR-15 Sporter II (bottom) both make good sniper rifles, and are shown with Tasco scopes and DTA Mil/Brakes. The H-BAR has an "improvised" cheek piece created from an old AR-15 stock and epoxy putty. The Sporter's plastic magazine makes an excellent monopad.

factory number CO6550), which is identical to the M16A2 except for its semiauto-only selector and lack of auto parts. The AR-15 A2 Sporter II (CO6500) is similar to the government version but lacks the finger-adjustable windage/elevation rear sights. The semiauto Sporter II H-BAR (Heavy Barrel—CO6600) offered by Colt also has the finger-adjustable rear sights and all the other features of the military H-BAR except for the burst mode.

There is a lot of confusion about the twists of the various AR-15 models. Very early rifles had a 1-in-14 twist which proved to be inaccurate, especially in cold weather. The 1-in-12 twist was used in all the A1 models and the civilian AR-15 Sporter. The new, and very effective, 1-in-7 twist is available with the new M16A2 and AR-15 A2 Sporter II rifles. It is first choice with all types of .223 ammunition due to its ability to operate with

a wide range of ammunition as well as the deadly break-up of the bullet upon impact caused by the faster twist.

Chamberings other than the .223 are also available for various AR-15 models, especially with some of the non-Colt versions. For those looking for a 9mm rifle for sniper use, Colt offers a complete 9mm carbine; SGW sells a 9mm conversion bolt/upper receiver/barrel kit which can be used with M16-style lower receivers with a front pushpin to create a 9mm carbine. SGW also offers barrels, upper receiver/barrel conversion kits, or compete AR-15 rifles chambered for the 6mm/.223 wildcat as well as similar conversion kits or rifles for the 7.62x39mm. SGW can also create barrels with special chamberings for those who wish to convert their AR-15 to some wildcat chambering.

The basic design of the AR-15 is very well thought out from an ergonomic standpoint, and all "controls" are easy to operate. The overall design allows the rifle to be relatively light even when equipped with a heavy barrel.

As with a number of other semiauto military rifles, the AR-15 is capable of excellent accuracy provided pressure is not placed on its barrel by a sling or bipod; doing so can change the point of impact. When using a sling or bipod, this should be kept in mind.

Probably the best mount being made for the AR-15 is the new A.R.M.S. mount. The unit has a see-through base to allow the user to quickly use the iron sights if necessary, and the base itself will accept Weaver rings as well as NATO standard scopes and night vision equipment. The A.R.M.S. base sells for about $39.

A huge number of parts and accessories exist for the AR-15, allowing a sniper to virtually customize the rifle to his tastes. The length of pull on stocks can be changed very easily by substituting various stocks for the one which came with the

Colt's AR-15 9mm Carbine is based on Colt's Commando version of the AR-15. Shooters used to the AR-15 will find that the 9mm Carbine operates identically. Photo courtesy of Colt Industries.

The excellent Aimpoint scope mount is shown on the AR-15 A2 H-BAR. Note its adjustable rear sight and cartridge buffer to the rear of the ejection port.

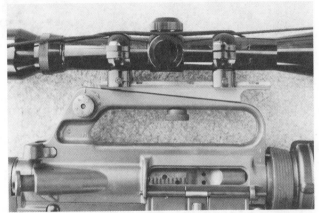

The new A.R.M.S. mount for the AR-15 has a see-through base so that the user can quickly use the iron sights if need be.

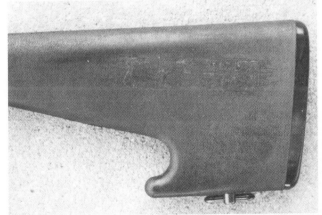

Providing a convenient hand hold when a bipod is used on the AR-15, Choate Machine and Tool's E2 stock is three-quarters of an inch longer than the A1 stock.

rifle. Many tall shooters find the stock of the A1 models of the AR-15 to be about an inch too short, while short shooters using the A2 model may find it too long (it is three-quarters of an inch longer than the A1 model).

If the A1 stock is taken as the "standard" length, three-quarters of an inch can be added to the rifle's length of pull by substituting the Colt A2 factory stock or Choate Machine and Tool's Zytel E2 stock, both of which are three-quarters of an inch longer than the standard stock. The A1 stock can also be lengthened (at a bit lower cost) by adding a Choate extended butt plate (which replaces the trap door of the AR-15), or by using an SGW stock spacer kit (which goes between the receiver and the stock).

Length can also be added to any of these stocks

The "kit" for Colt's Delta H-BAR rifle consists of an H-BAR AR-15 A2, Colt cheek mount, A.R.M.S. scope mount, and a rubber-armored 3-9x power-variable Tasco scope in a carrying case. Photo courtesy of Colt Industries.

by using the slip-on butt pad available from E & L Manufacturing. These pads cost only about $15 and fit all variations of the stock, thereby adding between one-quarter and one-half an inch to the length of pull. Best of all, the pad itself has a small insert which can be removed allowing only an additional one-quarter inch to be added to the stock; this is especially useful where a different length of pull is needed when switching from heavy to light clothing or vice versa.

Some snipers prefer the "heads up" use of the scoped AR-15 while others will benefit from the use of a cheek pad. Currently, Colt is offering a cheek pad which is fastened to a standard stock by means of several bolts. It is also possible to make a "custom" cheek pad by cutting out a section of an old AR-15 stock. The piece is mounted to the rifle with an epoxy putty filler to bring it to the proper height according to the sniper's tastes. This makes a very inexpensive and reliable cheek pad. Other sources of cheek rests include the Cherokee cheek rest and leather pads designed for Garand and M14 sniper/match use, available from Springfield Armory.

For sniper use, the trigger on the AR-15 has good and bad points. One plus is that the travel of the single-stage trigger is short, unlike that of many other military rifles. Normally, the pull of the AR-15 is around seven pounds; this weight can be dropped considerably if the trigger and hammer are polished and deburred a bit by a qualified gunsmith. This done, the trigger pull becomes ideal for a sniper rifle.

The H-BAR version of the AR-15 A2 currently offered by Colt has a barrel which is heavy enough to allow the use of a bipod or sling without causing a change in bullet impact; the barrel soaks up more heat during repeated shots, making it a first choice for those looking for an out-of-the-box sniper rifle. Colt also offers a "package" for police/military snipers called the Delta H-BAR rifle. This consists of an H-BAR AR-15 A2 with the new finger-adjustable rear sights of the H-BAR, plus a Colt cheek mount and A.R.M.S. scope mount, and a rubber-armored 3-9x power variable Tasco scope in a heavy carrying case. The rifle itself is reworked in Colt's "Custom Shop" department to assure its accuracy to within 1 MOA. The package carries a competitive price tag and makes it possible to get a complete sniper rifle with one purchase.

SGW also offers AR-15 H-BAR barrels which are quite accurate. In addition to standard-length

SGW offers AR-15 H-BAR barrels (shown here on an SGW rifle) which are quite accurate. While reducing muzzle noise, the twenty-four-inch barrel also boosts the bullet's velocity.

twenty-inch barrels, SGW offers longer twenty-four-inch barrels. These greatly reduce the muzzle noise of the rifle and boost the velocity of the bullet somewhat (longer barrels do not, in and of themselves, increase accuracy). SGW's Match barrels are capable of sub-MOA accuracy and are available in both standard steel and stainless steel.

SGW also markets a fluted match barrel which has the rigidity of a heavy barrel without its weight. Such a barrel should appeal to many of those destined to carry a sniper rifle around for extended periods. Because the fluting increases the surface area of the fluted barrel, heat build-up isn't as great as it is with many lighter barrels.

Another interesting creation from SGW is the International Match Upper Receiver, which is formed without the carrying handle/rear sight assembly. Instead, a Weaver-style scope base is molded into the top of the receiver, making it practical to mount a scope on the rifle without the need of a cheek rest. Like other SGW receivers, this one has the M16-style front pushpins, which make it possible to quickly disassemble the rifle for easier transportation or storage. (SGW also offers an adjustable rear "iron" target sight which can be mounted on the scope rails and a target front sight with interchangeable blade inserts.) Retail cost for the SGW Match receiver is about $110, with a kit consisting of match barrel assembly, receiver, and charging handle to create a whole upper receiver selling for about $492.

SGW will also assemble an AR-15 according to the buyer's specifications or will sell only the barrel, a few parts, or complete rifle kits so that a purchaser or armorer can either modify existing AR-15 rifles or build one from scratch.

Another variation on the H-BAR AR-15 theme is the Insight Systems, Inc. Model I sniper kit, which gives the ultimate in AR-15 accuracy to date. The kit consists of an upper receiver/barrel assembly by Insight Systems which can be used to replace the upper barrel/receiver of a standard AR-15, thereby transforming it into a .223 sniper weapon. The Insight system uses a heavy barrel which is free-floated inside a tough (but soft-to-the-touch) handguard. This much-needed floating of the barrel makes it possible to use a tight sling hold or mount a Harris bipod on the fore grip's sling swivels studs without any worry about changing the point of impact. The Insight Systems assembly uses the original weapon's bolt, carrier, and charging handle, which are readily exchanged from the rifle's original barrel/receiver assembly.

Insight Systems offers a number of "custom" options for barrel lengths (16-, 18-, 20-, 22-, and 24-inch barrels are available), chamberings (.223, 5.56mm NATO, or 6mm/.223 among others), twist rates, and use of an AR-15 or M16-style receiver, making it possible to create a rifle suited to a sniper's needs. Additionally, the Model I is made without front or rear iron sights and carrying handle; instead, a Weaver-style scope mount is placed low on the receiver. This arrangement makes a lot of sense with a sniper rifle and does away with the need for a cheek pad, since the scope is in line with the stock. Good shooters can cover a five-shot, one-hundred-yard group with a dime with the Insight Systems' barrel/receiver! (The author's personal experience has been that good ammunition can regularly produce three-quarter-inch groups at one hundred yards with the Insight System Model I. Some skilled shooters claim to be able to shoot three-eighth-inch groups!) For those wanting to milk the last bit of accuracy out of an AR-15, Insight is also offering a Match Rifle version of the Model I.

One of the best parts of the Insight Systems kit is that a whole rifle doesn't need to be purchased, only such parts as an upper receiver, handguard, or barrel. This keeps the price of the units down, with the standard Model I selling for about $530 and the Match Rifle going for approximately $800. For those who already have access to an AR-15 or M16, this translates into quite a savings over purchasing a second separate sniper rifle. Despite almost no advertising on the part of Insight Systems, a number of SWAT units are now using these in the U.S.

After seeing the accuracy which the Colt standard AR-15s, H-BAR rifles, SGW Match rifles, and Insight Systems kits are capable of, one can't help but think that the days of the bolt-action sniper rifle are probably numbered as far as many police and military users are concerned.

AR70

The AR70 is manufactured by the Pietro Beretta Company of Italy and is available in a number of models. The standard AR70 rifle is good enough to be used as a sniper rifle and an H-BAR version (the AR70/78, which was designed for use as a Squad Automatic Weapon) might be adapted to sniper use as well. Currently, a 1-in-12 twist is used, with the barrels dictating the use of lighter bullets, although at the time of this writing, Beretta is believed to be working on a new version of this rifle which will accept the AR-15/M16 magazine and which will have a faster twist rate.

The AR70 can be easily disassembled for cleaning and has a tough black epoxy finish for ease of maintenance. About the only drawbacks with the rifle are that its safety operates "backwards" from that of many other assault rifles and the rifle is rather heavy. Most will find these are minor considerations (since the selector can be being modified by a gunsmith).

The AR70 rifle has steel scope-blocks welded to the receiver top so that a scope is easily mounted in a low position on the rifle. Beretta currently sells a scope and bipod for the rifle as well as a night-vision scope. For those who find the fixed mounts don't allow for proper eye relief, B-Square also offers a mount which allows the use of standard rings in a variety of positions.

AUG

The AUG (Armee Universal Gewehr [rifle]) is a high-tech .223 assault rifle manufactured by Steyr-Daimler-Puch, AG, of Austria. It has become the main assault rifle of Austria and Australia, and has been adopted by Malaysia, Morocco, Oman, Saudia Arabia, and Tunisia. The rifle has seen limited use by elite units like the U.S. Navy SEALs and the British SAS (Special Air Service), as well as some police teams in the U.S.

The AUG has a lot of plastic parts (including a plastic trigger group and stock), as well as a bullpup design (which some shooters dislike because it places the face close to the ejection port). The standard series of AUG rifles have quick-change barrels of various lengths and can be quickly field-stripped by hand (they can even be detail-stripped with only a few common tools). Unfortunately, the built-in 1.5 scope in the rifle's carrying handle makes

This close-up of the AR-70 shows a B-Square scope mount attached to the scope-mount blocks welded to the top of the rifle. The scope is a Bushnell Banner adjustable power scope. Photo courtesy of B-Square.

While the standard AUG (shown here) is only marginal as a sniper rifle because of its 1.5x power scope, the HBAR-T model would be ideal for sniper use. Photo courtesy of Gunsouth.

the standard rifle unsuitable for most sniper uses.

One version of the rifle doesn't have the built-in scope, however. This exception is the 24.4-inch HBAR-T (Heavy Barrel Automatic Rifle-Telescope base) version of the rifle. This version lends itself to sniper use since it has a special receiver which can use removable telescopic scopes or night-vision equipment. The HBAR-T usually has a special carrying handle which mounts on the upper scope ring halves; many snipers may wish to remove this handle since, even though it is quite strong, extended use of the handle may throw the scope zero off slightly.

As with other versions of the AUG, the HBAR-T has a chrome-lined chamber and barrel. The flash suppressor on the 24.5-inch barrel is available in an M16 style or a specially designed muzzle brake and compensator with two large ports on each side and three smaller holes drilled into its front. The standard version of the HBAR-T also has a bipod mounted just behind the flash hider; it folds up under the barrel when not in use. Steyr also offers a night-vision scope as an option with their HBAR-T.

While the HBAR-T was not available for testing at the time of this writing, it appears that the rifle is accurate enough for sniper use. In addition to selective-fire models, semiauto AUG rifles are also available. AUG rifles are being imported to the United States by Gunsouth.

Chinese Type 79

The People's Republic of China has adopted the Dragunov design as the basis for its Type 79 sniper rifle. The two rifles are virtually identical, down to the use of the same antiquated 7.62x54mmR cartridge. Currently, the rifle is being exported by Poly Technologies, Inc., in China as its PDM-86 rifle.

While the Type 79 is a fair sniper rifle, it is only passable compared to modern Western designs which are capable of greater accuracy and are chambered for more suitable cartridges. (For more information about the Dragunov design, see below.)

Dragunov

The Soviet Snayperskaya Vinyovka Dragunov (self-loading rifle, Dragunov) was created to replace the M1891/30 Mosin-Nagant bolt-action sniper rifle. Although Yevgeniy Feodorovich Dragunov is credited with developing the rifle in the late 1950s, the rifle in fact borrows heavily from the Kalashnikov design and differs only in a few minor points (including its chambering for the old M1891 7.62x54mmR cartridge). The Dragunov sniper rifle was adopted by the Soviet Army in 1963.

The decision to use an antiquated rimmed cartridge for the Dragunov was apparently made in order to use stocks of the shells which were on hand and which were also used in Soviet belt-fed machine guns. While a rimmed shell would seem a poor choice for semiauto design, the rifle seems to function well, partially due to its limited magazine.

The Kalashnikov trigger design has been simplified, since the sniper rifle fires only in semiauto mode. This has improved the weapon's trigger pull. The sniper rifle also uses a short-stroke gas piston to minimize the change in the rifle's balance during

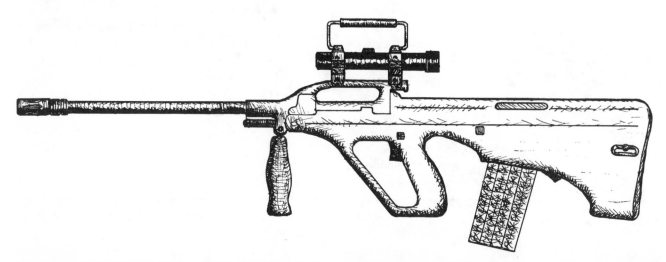

The Steyr AUG HBAR-T lends itself to sniper use since it has a special receiver which can handle removable telescopic scopes or night vision equipment. The HBAR-T usually has a special carrying handle which mounts on the upper scope ring halves.

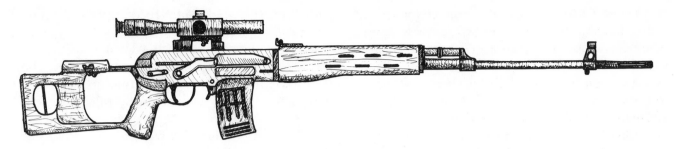

The Dragunov borrows heavily from the Kalashnikov design. It is chambered for the 7.62x56mmR cartridge. The Chinese Type 79 and Polish SVD are nearly identical to the Dragunov.

recoil; in theory, this makes the rifle a bit more accurate and quicker if a follow-up shot is needed.

The machined receiver has been strengthened for the more powerful cartridge, and the wooden stock has a skeletonized design which creates a pistol grip. The cheek rest is adjustable, but length of pull or other butt adjustments common on many other sniper rifles are unavailable. The barrel has iron sights similar to those of the AK-47 and ends with a long, fluted flash hider.

The barrel of the Dragunov is neither overly heavy nor fluted, so the rifle lacks some of the accuracy normally expected from a sniper rifle. Despite Soviet "hype" about the rifle's accuracy, groups from most rifles are believed to fall in the 1.5-2 MOA range, with some authorities feeling it is probably much worse given the poor quality of some Soviet ammunition. Nevertheless, it should be noted that within ranges of several hundred yards and with shots aimed at the torso, such a rifle would have the accuracy needed for sniper use.

The Soviets also produce a sporter rifle based on the Dragunov action known as the Medved (Bear). It has a slightly different receiver cover, a sport-style wooden stock, and a simplified scope.

The Dragunov scope mount fastens onto the left of the rifle's receiver to hold the scope in place. The scope currently in use is the PSO1, which has replaced the PU, PE, and SVT40 series of scopes. The 4x power PSO1 can detect active night-vision equipment (which sends out infrared light) thanks to an internal filter; with an infrared light source, the scope can double as a crude night-vision scope.

The scope's viewing field has one corner graduated so that the sniper can estimate the range to his target by bracketing a standing man. The ranging brackets are broken into one-hundred-meter increments and beyond 1,000 yards—perhaps a little optimistic, given the accuracy potential of the rifle. A battery is used to power a small electric

bulb in the scope which illuminates the reticles in dim light.

While the Dragunov sniper rifle doesn't blaze any trails in new technology, it is simple to produce and maintain. Its rugged design allows the Soviets to produce large numbers of the weapons quickly and cheaply. Since Soviet military doctrine places importance on the deployment of the sniper, the Dragunov would seem to suit Soviet needs quite well.

FN LAR (FN FAL)

The Fabrique Nationale d'Armes de Guerre (National Factory for Arms of War) in Belgium created the FAL (Fusil Automatique Leger or, as translated into English, LAR—Light Automatic Rifle) and marketed it in 1950. Except for a few experimental rifles, all are chambered for the .308 Winchester. The rifle has a number of features that appeal to those looking for a modern sniper weapon including a pistol grip, 20-round magazine, and heavy barrel versions capable of good accuracy.

Because the rifle has been adopted in the past by many countries (including Argentina, Austria, Belgium, Canada, Chile, Ecuador, England, India, Israel, the Netherlands, and South Africa), a wide variety of parts and accessories is available for these rifles. (Care must be taken to determine whether metric or English measurements are used on a rifle before purchasing parts for it; not even magazines are interchangeable.) Because each country has its own ideas of what constitutes an ideal combat rifle, there is a wide range of styles of FN LARs, with wooden and plastic furniture, folding stocks, scopes, sights, bipods, and other accessories available to meet each country's requirements.

One of the more interesting FN LAR versions available to the sniper is the HBAR (heavy-barreled) version, which is nearly identical to the standard version (though generally having a bipod as well as a heavier barrel). Originally designed for use as SAWs, the rifle often proved to be unreliable in the automatic mode and also lacked a quick-change barrel. However, the rifles have proven to be useful as sniper weapons, and many have been converted into nonselective fire rifles. (Fabrique Nationale classifies its heavy barrel version as its Model 50-41 FAL, having a plastic stock, while the wooden furniture HBAR version is the Model 50-42 FALO.)

The chamber and barrel of most FN LARs are chrome-lined. Maximum accuracy is usually achieved when the barrel is head-spaced to its minimum specifications (head space can be reduced on an FN LAR by replacing its locking shoulder and/or bolt). When head-spaced to minimum tolerances, many FN LARs are capable of 1 MOA accuracy.

In the U.S., Springfield Armory is importing an FN LAR as its SAR-48 series of rifles with a price tag that is considerably less than the European-made versions of the rifle. The company also sells a heavy barrel version of the rifle from original military parts built around Springfield's forged receiver; this version comes with a bipod and has wooden furniture on it. Currently, the SAR-48 is the most competitively priced of the FN LAR rifles and offers a lot of value for the money. Springfield Armory, which also offers a large number of accessories (as well as a .22 LR version of the SAR-48) and spare

parts for its rifles, is capable of servicing them should such work be needed.

Israeli-made FN LAR parts were imported into the U.S. by Armscorp of America for a time; the parts were then assembled into rifles in the States. Among the various versions of the rifle sold were two Match Heavy Barrel rifles (one with a bipod and the other without) which might be used as sniper rifles.

The FN bipod is designed to fit into grooves on the FN LAR handguard when the bipod is folded. Unfortunately, the bipod hangs toward the very front of the barrel. While HBAR versions of the FN LAR aren't as prone to barrel flex as standard models, the point of impact may change when a bipod is used on some FN LARs. Care should therefore be taken to determine whether this will happen before using the bipod-equipped rifle in a sniper capacity.

The location of the safety/selector switch is a little awkward for many users, especially those with small hands. This can generally be alleviated by cutting down the ridge on the upper edge of the handguard as well as grinding down the top of the stud on the receiver take-down release (having a gunsmith silver-solder an extension arm to the safety will complete the project if the first two steps don't completely solve the problem). For those used to the AR-15, grinding off the ridge in front of the magazine release allows the release of the magazine

This model of Springfield Armory's H-BAR version of the FN LAR comes with a bipod and wooden furniture. Photo courtesy of Gunsouth.

by the trigger finger; coupled with the same style of selector, this makes it possible to quickly switch from the AR-15 to the FN LAR without much confusion while under pressure.

The FN LAR rifle has a gas regulator that allows it to be used with a wide range of ammunition, making it ideal for snipers using hand loads. The regulator can also be adjusted for manual operation only so that the bolt won't cycle automatically; this might be of use with a silencer-equipped weapon firing subsonic loads. The regulator is located just ahead of the gas tube and can be adjusted with a screwdriver.

The FN LAR can also be "stripped" by several pounds to make it a bit lighter to carry. Removing the carrying handle (which is almost useless with a scope mounted on the rifle), sling swivels, iron sights, and handguards drops over 2 rounds from the rifle's weight. Since none of these parts are used in prone shooting, many snipers should consider removing them in order to shed unnecessary weight.

Fabrique Nationale markets a four-power scope for its rifles. The company also carries a "high" mount, which holds the scope over the receiver and above the iron sights, and a "low" mount, which holds the scope to the upper left of the receiver. Unfortunately, many mounts (including those created for British and Canadian military FN LARs) are very poor since they fasten to the removable receiver cover, which doesn't lock tightly in place. Firing such a scope mount often yields groups of 8-10 MOA!

Better scope bases are available from A.R.M.S., Armson, and Springfield Armory, with B-Square's lower receiver mounted scope base being among the best. (Interestingly, B-Square's mount is a bit less expensive than other contenders.)

Galil Sniper Rifle

Israel had adopted the FN LAR as its standard military weapon, but by the late 1960s, it found that the rifles didn't function as well as might be hoped for in harsh desert conditions.

As a stopgap measure, Israel started using M16 rifles imported from the United States. In the meantime, following the Arab/Israeli War of 1967, a number of captured AKs were tested and evaluated by the Israelis. Following testing, the decision was made to select a new rifle based on a Frankenstein-like test weapon which had been cobbled up from an AK receiver, M16 bolt and barrel, plus various Stoner 63 rifle parts. After making a number of modifications to the rifle, IMI (Israel Military Industries) started producing the AK variation in 1973 for use by the Israeli military. The weapon became known as the Galil (named after Israeli Galil, the principal designer behind the modified AK).

A number of the rifles were made for export. South Africa, the Netherlands, and other countries soon adopted the new Galil as their military rifles. Rifles made for export are chambered for the .223 Remington (used by the Israeli military) as well as the .308 Winchester.

The Israelis had been using accurized M14 rifles for sniping purposes. Therefore, it was a logical jump to adopt the Galil rifles chambered for the .308

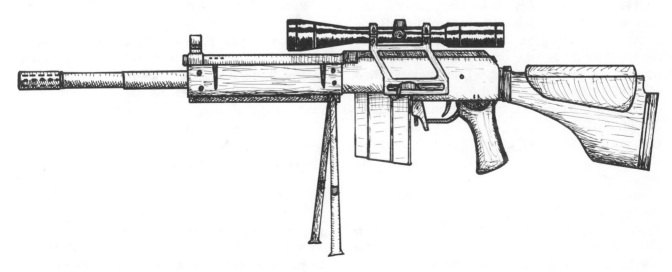

The Galil sniper rifle has a heavy barrel with an FN-FAL style muzzle brake. The bipod is mounted in front of the receiver and its legs fold forward under the fore grip when not in use.

as their new sniper rifle. This also made training and repair of the rifles easier because the design was nearly identical to that of the M14.

The Galils used for sniping have heavy barrels and usually have brakes mounted on them (a silencer is available for use with subsonic ammunition). As with many other rifles, the Galil has a slight tendency to shift its point of impact when a bipod is placed on its barrel; therefore, the Israelis mounted the bipod just in front of the receiver, with the legs folding forward under the fore grip when not in use. The stock is still capable of being folded (as is the case with the other versions of the Galil), but it is made of wood rather than the tubular metal stock found on the standard military rifle. The sniper stock has an adjustable comb and a heavy rubber butt plate.

The Nimrod ranging scope (made in Israel) is used with the Galil. The scope is mounted offset to the left of the receiver, thereby making left-handed shooting nearly impossible. Iron sights are kept on the rifle for emergency use or for use at close ranges.

The Galil rifles are dependable but not without their human engineering faults: the triggers have a tendency to pinch the shooting finger, and the Kalashnikov-style safety makes a rather alarmingly loud click. The Galil also flings its brass quite a distance, often putting a large dent in the cartridges. As a result, those snipers planning to reload their practice rounds will want to get the optional brass catcher and ejection port buffer.

Heckler & Koch PSG1, G3SG1, HK-94SG1

Heckler & Koch rifles can be traced back to the German StG44 of World War II. The rifles all use a roller bolt-locking system which does away with the need for a gas tube or piston. West Germany adopted the CETME rifle as its G1, but later switched to the FN LAR (designated the G2). The FN LAR didn't prove to be what the Germans wanted, though, so they modified the CETME to the current G3 specifications, and a new German company, Heckler & Koch, was created to manufacture the rifles.

Since its introduction, the G3 rifle has gone through several minor design changes (in regard to stocks, sights, and the addition of a flash hider). The German military rifle produced now is the G3A3, although it is generally referred to simply as the G3 rifle. A number of variations of the rifle have been adopted by other countries as well.

Capable of very good accuracy, this HK-91 "sniper" sports a Trijicon scope, DTA Mil/ Brake, and improvised cheek piece. The removal of the front handguard lowered the rifle's total weight by one pound.

The G3 rifle proved to be very tough and reliable, and Heckler & Koch has aggressively sought new markets for its products. Because of this, the company has created whole families of similar rifles modeled after the G3, with different chamberings, barrel configurations, and stocks available to suit nearly any needs which might exist in the way of small arms. In the process, the company has created several very fine sniper rifles.

In the family of rifles chambered for the .308 Winchester/7.62mm NATO cartridge, one version of the rifle which often was pressed into service as a sniper rifle was the G3A3Z. This rifle was simply a standard G3 with a scope mounted on it.

A step up from the G3A3Z sniper is the G3SG1, which is a G3 with a match-grade barrel, a bipod, an adjustable cheek-piece stock, 5-round magazine, set trigger, and Zeiss 1.5-6x power variable scope mounted on it.

Recently, the G3SG1 has more or less been replaced by the PSG-1 sniper rifle. The "Prazisions-schutzengewehr 1" (precision-shooter's rifle)— mercifully shortened to the PSG-1—has a heavy, free-floated barrel inside the rifle's fore grip. The barrel is devoid of a flash hider and uses a polygonal twist rather than standard rifling. The rifle comes with a tripod on which the shooter can rest the fore grip, with the tripod's top fitting into the rail on the lower side of the fore grip.

The PSG1's trigger pull is set at 3.2 pounds with an over-travel boot attached to the trigger. All but the early models of the PSG1 have a stippled pistol grip with a wide rest on its base. The stock has a pivoted butt plate which can be adjusted for length of pull, and the cheek piece is adjustable as well. Originally, the PSG1 had walnut furniture; most production models now use plastic.

Heckler & Koch has created a very large number of accessories for its rifles. If a compact sniper rifle in .223 were needed, for example, the addition of the H&K telescoping stock (shown here on the HK-93), in addition to a scope, would do the trick. Photo courtesy of Heckler & Koch.

HK-33 rifles are capable of good accuracy and can be pressed into service as sniper rifles with the addition of Heckler & Koch's scope-mounting system. Shown is the semiauto HK-93. Photo courtesy of Heckler & Koch.

A bolt forward-assist device similar to that of the AR-15 A2/M16 is located just behind the ejection port of the PSG1; it is designed to allow the sniper to cycle the bolt back and chamber a round from the magazine while quietly "riding" the charging lever forward (rather than releasing it). The final seating and closing of the bolt are achieved by using the forward assist. (How often this would be needed is uncertain, though it would surely be a much-needed option when quiet operation was essential.)

The rifle generally comes with a Hensoldt 6x power scope with an illuminated duplex reticle for low-light shooting. The rifle has no iron sights, since the scope mount is welded to the top of the receiver to avoid its working loose; the mount can also be used with equipment conforming to the STANAG 2324 dimensions. With quality ammunition, the PSG1 is capable of shooting 1 MOA or smaller groups.

The .223/5.56mm HK-33 family of rifles includes the HK-33SG1 sniper rifle, which was also given the G3SG1 designation since its principal difference

The H&K PSG-1 comes with a tripod on which the rifle's fore grip can rest while the tripod's top fits into the rail on the fore grip's lower side. Photo courtesy of Heckler & Koch.

Shown here is the silencer-equipped MP5SD2. Photo courtesy of Heckler & Koch.

from the .308 rifle was mainly that of chambering with a few minor differences in dimensions; the HK-33SG1 had the adjustable cheek rest and set trigger of the larger .308 version of the rifle. The HK-33SG1, like other rifles in the HK-33 family, has a 1-in-12 twist suited to the lighter .223 bullets.

With the adoption of the new SS-109 round by NATO, a new model of rifle, the G41, has been introduced by Heckler & Koch. The HK-41 has a magazine well/latch designed to accept the AR-15/M16 magazine (as well as the Heckler & Koch magazine designed for the rifle), a forward assist, different trigger group/pistol grip, and new fore grip. Additionally, the barrel has a 1-in-7 twist, making it more accurate and more lethal with a wide range of .223 cartridges.

A G41 with a good barrel (like many of the newer Western assault rifles) is capable of 1 MOA accuracy with quality ammunition. Because of this, a G41 fitted with a scope would make a good sniper rifle. Possibly with this in mind, the G41 has Weaver-like bases welded to the top of its receiver which allow the use of a the NATO Steiner scope as well as other scopes made to use the mounts.

Included in Heckler & Koch's 9mm submachine gun family are some long-barreled carbines. These carbines, when coupled with the scope mounts designed for them, might serve as short-range sniper rifles for those wanting such a weapon. Best suited for such use is the silencer-equipped MP5SD2 (with a standard stock) and MP5SD3 (with retractable stock), or the 16-inch barrel semiauto carbine marketed as the HK-94 in the U.S. (For those seeking a suppressor for the HK-91, Jonathan Arthur Ciener offers excellent suppressors for Heckler & Koch carbines.)

At the time of this writing, Heckler & Koch is offering a version of its semiauto HK-94, the HK-94SG1, with a Harris bipod, an adjustable cheek stock (similar to that of the G3SG1), a flash hider, and a 6x power Leupold scope fitted with the old claw mount developed for the G3 rifle. As with other 9mm carbines, accuracy is not on par with rifle-caliber guns; groups of 3 MOA are about the best that the rifle can achieve with quality ammunition. However, given the fact that such a sniper weapon would be deployed at close ranges, this accuracy would seem to be acceptable for such use.

Since all these weapons are based on the G3, the positions of the selector and charging lever are nearly identical from one weapon to the next, making them ideal for police or military units interested in adopting a common family of rifles in order to simplify training and maintenance needs. Most AR-15 users will also become quickly comfortable with the Heckler & Koch rifles since the safeties and magazine releases of the two different rifle families are in nearly identical positions.

Heckler & Koch rifles have a good reputation for reliability and always seem to have minimal parts breakage. While brass cartridges fired from the weapon become "fluted" or scored, they are still reloadable (and buffers are available to keep the brass from flying too far from the shooter).

Two small weaknesses of the rifles, though, are the selector lever, which is just a tad awkward to reach for those with small hands, and the magazine release on the semiauto versions (HK-91, HK-93, HK-94), which is impossible to reach without the shooter removing his hand from the pistol grip. The charging handle on the pre-HK-41 rifles is also hard to operate when the action is "locked" on an empty chamber, and all but the HK-41 lack a bolt hold-open device. Nevertheless, these are rather small considerations compared to the overall quality of the rifles.

Those modifying standard HK-91, HK-93, or HK-94 rifles for sniper use may wish to have the trigger reworked by Williams Trigger Specialties in order to smooth its pull and lower the weight of the pull. Currently, H&K is also selling the pistol grip/trigger group of their sniper rifle for use with the HK-91. This is an ideal way to upgrade the pull of an H&K rifle; the trigger groups are quickly exchanged

by field stripping the rifle. Williams can also create a special set trigger for the Heckler & Koch rifles.

Those using standard rifles may also want to change the length of pull on their rifles; this can be easily accomplished with an adjustable stock extension available from E & L Manufacturing. The butt plate adds from one-half inch to one-and-one-half inches to the pull.

Heckler & Koch scope mounts have a claw which fastens onto the top of the rifle's receiver to hold the scope in place. Those wanting to mount scopes other than those supplied by Heckler & Koch may wish to use an A.R.M.S. adapter bracket on the H&K scope mount. This will allow the sniper to mount any scope with Weaver rings as well as NATO standard scopes and night-vision equipment. Less expensive scope mounts are available from B-Square and Armson; these are both excellent mounts which allow the use of Weaver rings and carry low price tags.

In addition to the standard scopes available from Heckler & Koch for their rifles, the company also offers an infrared night-vision scope and a passive night-vision scope.

Polish SVD

The Polish SVD is a direct copy of the Soviet Dragunov and, as such, has little to distinguish it from the Soviet weapon.

Romanian FPK

The Romanian version of the Soviet AKM rifle is designed so that the bolt/bolt carrier travels farther than is necessary for the short 7.62x39mm

G3 rifles are often used as sniper rifles. The use of the Heckler & Koch claw mount, shown here on the semiauto HK-91, makes scope mounting quick. Photo courtesy of Heckler & Koch.

round. In 1980, Romanian designers took advantage of this feature to create a sniper rifle modeled after the basic AKM rifle. This was done by substituting a new barrel (with a special muzzle brake) on their rifle's receiver, changing the bolt face, lengthening the gas piston, adding a new laminated wood skeletonized stock to the rifle, creating a new shortened magazine, and adding two new reinforcement plates to the receiver for added strength.

While in theory the Romanian FPK's long-stroke piston should make the rifle less accurate than the Dragunov's short-stroke system, it doesn't seem to be detrimental to accuracy in practice. The FPK scope rides on a special mount on the left side of the rifle in the same manner as the Dragunov scope.

Ruger Mini-14

The Mini-14 is chambered for the .223 and is a little brother to the U.S. M14 rifle. It is also an improved version over the original since the gas port and piston have been redesigned, and parts of the receiver and trigger group have been strengthened.

Unfortunately, the Mini-14—like many other military-style rifles—doesn't have the tight accuracy needed for a sniper weapon as it comes out of the box. The rifle is capable of being accurized to within 1 MOA, however, making it a candidate for sniper use, especially with law-enforcement groups that have adopted the Mini-14 as their standard issue rifle. The huge variety of aftermarket accessories available for the Mini-14 also makes it a good choice for those wishing to modify the rifle to suit their needs.

Improving the Mini-14's accuracy generally consists of replacing the factory barrel with a heavy barrel and modifying the gas system to fit the wider diameter of the new barrel. Such work is currently done by Accuracy Rifle Systems. Barrels are available with twists from 1-in-14 through 1-in-7; stainless-steel barrels as well as standard steel barrels are also offered by Accuracy Rifle Systems.

The most suitable model of the Mini-14 for such modification is usually the Ranch Rifle version, which has integral scope mounts molded into its receiver. However, the standard models of the rifle can accept the excellent scope mounts marketed by B-Square if the user so desires. (Accuracy Rifle Systems will also modify the trigger pull of the Mini-14, drill and tap the receiver for scope mounts, and perform other custom work.)

At the time of this writing, sources close to Sturm, Ruger & Company say that the company is considering adding a heavy-barrel, "varminter" Mini-14 to its lineup. Should such a rifle become available, it would make an ideal sniper rifle for those familiar with the standard Mini-14 or M14 rifles, or for those looking for an inexpensive, semiauto sniper rifle.

The Mini-14, with its low initial price tag, makes a very inexpensive alternative (even when subject to custom work) to those wanting a sniper rifle in .223.

Sterling AR-180 SCS

For a short time during the late 1970s, Sterling Armaments Company in England produced the AR-180 rifle through a license from Armalite. Unfortunately, Sterling Armaments seemed to have trouble with quality control, and many of the rifles

With an Accuracy Rifle Systems barrel, the Mini-14 makes an ideal sniper rifle capable of shooting 1 MOA groups. Shown is the Ranch Rifle with its integral scope mounts. Photo courtesy of Sturm, Ruger & Company.

produced were far from perfect. This, coupled with the overwhelming acceptance of the AR-15/M16 by civilians and the law-enforcement and military communities in the United States, spelled the end to AR-180 production.

During the period in which Sterling produced the AR-180, the company also produced five hundred modified AR-180 sniper rifles for use by Britain's Special Police Forces. These rifles used a fixed stock (rather than a folding stock like the standard AR-180), with a Monte Carlo hump to the stock and a modified thumb hole pistol grip. The fore grip actually extended back around the receiver to join the stock and pistol grip, thereby creating a unit which minimized the amount of flex placed on the barrel when pressure was placed against the stock.

Possibly the major problem of the Sterling design was that the rifle had the standard-length, standard-sized AR-180 barrel rather than a longer heavy barrel. Undoubtedly, this made the AR-180 SCS less accurate than it might have been with a heavy barrel and possibly contributed to the lack of acceptance of the AR-180 SCS by those needing a sniper rifle.

In short, the AR-180 SCS had little to offer in the realm of sniper rifles and is not currently in production.

U.S. M1

During World War II, the U.S. military worked to produce a sniper rifle to replace the 1903A4 bolt-action sniper rifle, which was based on the old Springfield rifle. The final outcome of this work was the M1C and M1D sniper rifles, which were based on the Garand rifle. The basic difference between the two versions is the "quick detach" design of the scope mounts; the M1C has two levers, while the M1D has one.

Lyman Alaskan 2.2x power hunting scopes were mounted on both versions of the rifle, along with a cheek pad (a necessity, thanks to the mounting of the scope on the left of the receiver) and a flash hider which fastened to the bayonet stud. The M1C saw extensive use during World War II, while the M1D was more commonly used during the Korean War.

While the Garand rifle is not as inherently accurate as many more modern rifles (many feel this is because the gas piston hole is placed near the muzzle of the rifle), the guns are capable of good accuracy with glass-bedded, quality barrels. Currently, Springfield Armory is offering more

accurate versions of the Garand rifles known as National Match and Ultra Match guns. Springfield Armory also offers collectors a reproduction of the M1D sniper rifle with an authentic M84 scope and various other accessories found on the original.

While the Garands were good in their day, the old .30-06 rifles don't have the inherent accuracy of most modern sniper rifles. They are therefore of more interest from a historic perspective than for use as modern sniper weapons.

U.S. M21 RIFLE

The M14 was originally developed as a replacement for the U.S. Garand rifle (and, as such, can be thought of as a greatly improved variant of the Garand). While the M14 proved to be less than ideal in many ways as the standard infantry rifle, the sniper variations proved to be quite deadly on the battlefields of Vietnam.

In 1968, the U.S. Army ordered the Army Materiel Command to create 1,800 special M14 rifles for sniper use. The rifles' accuracy was improved according to the methods developed by the U.S. Army Marksmanship Training Unit at Fort Benning and equipped with the Redfield 3-9x hunting scope. This scope had been modified according to the specifications of James Leatherwood so that it could be used for an automatic ranging/bullet-drop compensation system as well as for targeting. (Interestingly, the scope mount was designed so that the scope could be readily mounted to any M14 rifle, thereby making it possible to quickly transform a rifle in the field into a make-do sniper rifle.)

These 1,800 rifles proved to be very effective in Vietnam and the rifle had its experimental designation, the XM21, changed to its current M21 in 1975. During the late 1970s, the U.S. Army did work toward creating a product-improved M21 as well as creating specifications for a Future Army Sniper Rifle System. This work, however, seems to have been discontinued without any determination having been made as to what was needed.

Recently the U.S. Army has decided to replace the M21 with a modified bolt-action Remington 700, which will be designed as the M24 sniper rifle. This will bring the Army's rifle back full circle to the bolt action operation. (The exact reasons for this change are uncertain, but sources close to the U.S. military believe it was because the M14 proved to be difficult to maintain and often suffered from poor accuracy after extended use in the field.)

Modern M1 Garands made by Springfield Armory make good sniper rifles when equipped with Ultra Match barrels. The top three rifles are standard versions; fourth from the top is a Garand with an ART IV scope. The bottom photo is of the Springfield M1-D. Photo courtesy of Springfield Armory, Inc.

For the police and civilian markets, Springfield Armory, Inc., offers a number of semiauto versions of the M14 rifle as the M1A, several excellent M21 versions of the rifle, and Match rifles capable of being used in a sniper role. Springfield also sells an "ART IV" scope for the rifle, as well as such accessories as M14-style bipods and slings. At the time of this writing, it appears that several U.S. police departments are equipping their SWAT groups with either the M1A or the M21.

In addition to standard stocks, Springfield also offers the M14A1 or E2-style stock, which affords the shooter a pistol grip for greater control of the rifle.

A wide range of barrels is also available from Springfield Armory with both 1-in-10 twists for lighter .308 bullets and 1-in-12 twists suitable for heavier bullets. (Generally, lighter bullets are more suitable for sniper work since they give a flatter trajectory, though some shooters may prefer heavier bullets.)

Springfield's new M21 has a glass-bedded walnut stock with an adjustable cheek pad and rubber recoil pad. The rifle also comes with a removable bipod mounted on its heavy Douglas barrel. Six 20-round magazines, a sling, and a cleaning kit also come with the rifle, which is test-fired and guaranteed to fire 1 MOA when it is sold. The scope and its mount can be quickly detached should the iron sights of the rifle need to be used.

The M14/M21 design, especially the newest generation, is quite strong. However, one potential weak link is the sear; care must be taken not to dry-fire the rifle or pull the trigger when the bolt is not locked since either action may damage the sear.

Great care should also be taken not to fire "hot" loads from any of the M14 variants since this can

Springfield Armory's M1A, shown with Springfield's ART IV scope, is ideal as a sniper rifle, especially with a match barrel. Photo courtesy of Springfield Armory, Inc.

Springfield's new M21 is shown with a glass-bedded walnut stock with adjustable cheek pad, rubber recoil pad, and removable bipod. Photo courtesy of Springfield Armory, Inc.

bend the operating rod. While the rifle may still function properly, a bent guide will often greatly degrade the rifle's accuracy.

Except for these minor design quirks, most of the bugs have since been worked out of the M14/M1A/M21 rifle family so that it is extremely dependable, and each makes an ideal sniper rifle.

Valmet M78/83S

After World War II, the USSR pressured the Allies into placing a ban on Finland which prevented the Finns from producing any small arms of their own. After the Allies' ban was lifted in the late 1950s, the Finns started producing a modified AK for their own use as a rifle and light machine gun as well as for export. The principal work done in developing and producing the Finnish weapons was—and continues to be—carried out by Valmet, a government-owned combine.

Between 1958 and 1960, a number of rifles was created around the AK design and tested by the Finns. In 1962, a version of the experimental rifle was adopted for military use.

By 1976, Valmet had produced the M76 family of rifles for the export market. The rifles are offered in .223 Remington, 7.62x39mm, and .308 Winchester chamberings. In 1978, the M78 LMG, with an integral bipod mounted to its long barrel, was added to the group. A bit later, a nearly identical rifle with a slightly modified stock and scope mount was included in the Valmet line as the M78/83S sniper rifle.

Both the M78 LMG and M78/83S are offered in .308 Winchester/7.62mm NATO chambering (with a few M78s having been made in .223), and the

The Valmet M78 LMG with integral bipod is nearly identical to the M78/83S sniper rifle. It is shown with a Tasco scope.

semiauto versions make excellent sniper rifles. Valmet offers scope mounts for the rifles along with the M76 scope mount adapter which fits on the M78 and M78/83S rifles. M78 and M78/83S barrels have excellent prong flash hiders which minimize flash in low-light conditions, and the iron sights have glow-in-the-dark inserts for emergency use at night.

For those who reload their practice rounds, a buffer which slips into the rear of the ejection port of the Valmet rifles is available, to minimize damage to cartridges during ejection and to limit their travel.

Internally, the Valmet rifles are nearly identical in their design to other AKs. Both externally and internally, overall fit and finish are much better than those of most communist rifles, making the Valmet rifles first choice among the various AK types.

Walther WA2000

The WA2000 is a departure from the usual semiauto sniper rifle design in that it is not a modified military rifle, having been designed specifically for sniper use. The rifle uses a bullpup

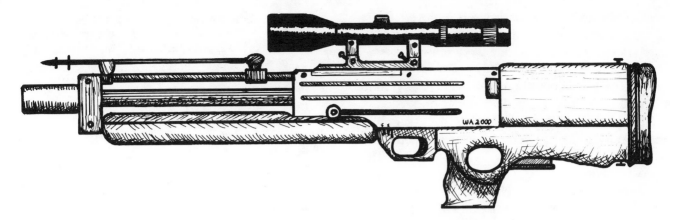

The bullpup-style WA2000 has a fluted barrel free-floated with its forward end resting on, but not restricted by, a rigid frame. The bipod can be slid up and down the top rail to suit the sniper's preference.

layout which gives it a long barrel with a short overall length; the negative side to this design is the placement of the shooter's cheek over the receiver and near the ejection port—something some snipers find hard to get used to.

The barrel is fluted and free-floated with its forward end resting on, but not restricted by, a rigid frame. The lower half of the frame has the fore grip mounted to it and the upper half has a folding bipod attached. The bipod can be slid back and forth along the upper frame rail according to the shooter's taste. It can then be locked into place.

The barrel is exposed to aid in cooling, and is fitted with a muzzle brake. An adjustable cheek rest is placed over the rifle's receiver, and an adjustable, heavy rubber butt plate covers the end of the rifle. Originally, wooden furniture was used on the rifle, but it is believed that a plastic stock and fore grip will be used in the near future. The rifle's bolt and cheek pad can be reversed so that cases eject from the left side of the receiver for left-handed shooters.

The trigger pull is adjustable and set at the factory between 2.7 to 3.2 pounds and the pistol grip has a thumb-hole styling. The safety is placed on the lower side of the receiver just above the front of the trigger guard. The rifle is available in .300 Winchester Magnum, 7.5mm Swiss, and .308 Winchester.

The WA2000 is normally equipped with a Schmidt & Bender 2.5-10x variable scope which is mounted on quick-release rings; a second scope mount is generally included with the rifle for use with night-vision equipment. Purchasers have the choice of carrying handle and slings that can be used with the rifle.

Yugoslavian M70 Series

The M70 series of rifles is based on the AK47/ AKM rifles, many of which are currently being exported. The heavy barrel models are sometimes used as sniper rifles and are available in .223 Remington and .308 Winchester (as well as the 7.62x39mm). With the addition of a scope, these rifles make fair sniper rifles, but their accuracy does not seem to be nearly as good as most Western sniper rifles. Semiauto, heavy barrel versions of these rifles are being imported into the U.S. by Mitchell Arms.

Yugoslavian M76

The Yugoslavians have chosen to use their standard AKM to create a sniper rifle chambered for the 7.92x57mm Mauser round (which was the round for their previous bolt-action sniper rifle as well as their machine gun). In theory, the long-stroke piston of the Yugoslavian M76 (as opposed to the short stroke of the Soviet Dragunov) causes some extra movement of the rifle which should translate into less accuracy; in practice, the system doesn't seem to be much less accurate than the short-stroke Dragunov rifles.

The teak wood furniture on the rifle is somewhat modified from the usual AK configuration; the pistol grip is fuller, and the stock has a sporter look to it, with a heavy rubber pad on the butt. The barrel itself is considerably longer than the standard AK barrel and uses a flash hider similar to that of the Soviet Dragunov.

The magazines used with the M76 hold the bolt open after the last shot is fired. Unfortunately, because the bolt lacks a hold-open device, the bolt crashes shut when the magazine is removed. Users of the rifle would probably be better off if the bolt-catch device on the magazine were removed.

While the trigger pull of the M76 is long and creepy, pull is generally in the 3.25 to 4 pound range, making it fairly good for sniper purposes.

The issue scope on the M76 is the 4x power PSO-1 optical sight, which is patterned after the Soviet PSO-1 used on the Dragunov rifle. The Yugoslav scope has one important improvement: it has a tritium illumination element in it which does away with the need for a battery-powered system. Older models of the PSO-1 also have an internal infrared detector which can be rotated into the viewing area of the scope; this unit causes an orange glow when it detects sources of infrared light from older styles of active night-vision devices. (With the use of newer, passive night-vision equipment becoming more widespread, newer versions of the PSO-1 are being made without the infrared filter.) A passive night-vision scope, the PN5X80(j) is also available for the M76. It uses rechargeable batteries and offers a 5x power magnification.

As with other communist-bloc sniper rifles, the M76's potential accuracy often suffers from poor-quality ammunition. However, even given quality ammunition, it is probable that the best accuracy the rifle can achieve is in the 1.5 MOA area, or perhaps worse. Thus, while the M76 is certainly capable of being used as a sniper rifle, it is not nearly as accurate as most Western sniper rifles.

Specifications for Assault Rifles

Name	Barrel Length (in.)	Weight Unloaded (lbs.)	Length (in.)	Magazine Capacity
AR-10	20	7.5[1]	40	20
AR-15 A1	20	6.31[1]	39	20, 30
AR-15 A2	20	7.88[1]	39.6	20, 30
AR-15 A2 (H-BAR)	20	8.62[1]	39.6	20, 30
AR-15 Delta H-BAR	20	10.25	39.6	20, 30
AR70	17.8	7.58[1]	37.6	5, 8, 30
AR70/78	17.8	11.7[1]	37.6	5, 8, 30
AUG	24	9.2[1]	35	30, 42
Chinese Type 79	24.5	9.46	48.2	10
Dragunov	24	9.5	48.2	10
FN LAR	21	9.4	43.5	20
Galil (.308)	21	17.6	43.8	20
HK-G3SG1	19.7	13.6	40.6	5, 20
HK-PSG1	25.6	17.8	47.5	5, 20
HK-33SG1	17.7	11	36.94	5, 20
HK-G41	18.9	8.5[1]	39.25	30
HK-94SG1	16.54	10.2	37	15
Polish SVD	24	9.5	48.2	10
Romanian FPK	21	10.69	45.5	10
Ruger Mini-14	18.5	6.5[1]	37.3	5, 20, 30
Sterling AR-180 SCS	18.25	6.7[1]	38	20
U.S. M1C/M1D	24	11.75	43.6	8
U.S. M14	22	8.7	44.1	20
U.S. M21	—			20
Valmet M78/83S	24.25	11	43.5	20
Walther WA2000	25.59	15.31	35.62	6
Yugoslav M70 HBAR	—			
Yugoslav M76	21.8	11.6	45.4	10

[1]Weight does not include scope.

6
Large-Caliber Rifles

Large-caliber rifles are a "new breed" that has emerged during the last few decades, mostly due to testing by the U.S. Army and the work of amateurs interested in long-range rifles. The idea of large-caliber rifles itself isn't new, however.

During the Civil War, it is believed that large-caliber Sharps buffalo rifles of .50 to .58 caliber, as well as large-bore scoped rifles used for target shooting, were used to snipe at enemies from extreme ranges. During World War I, there were suggestions that anti-tank weapons might be deployed as long-range sniper weapons. The optical systems of World War I, though, were far too crude to allow shooting at ranges much beyond the issue rifles of the day—which were considerably lighter than a large-caliber sniper rifle would be. Lack of a good muzzle brake design also kept the idea of a large sniper rifle from ever coming to fruition, since the gun had to be very heavy to avoid pounding the sniper apart during recoil. Only recently were optical systems and muzzle brakes perfected to the point where actual large-caliber rifles became practical.

The rounds used in modern large-caliber sniper rifles are far from new as well. Most modern large-caliber rifles are chambered for the .50-caliber BMG (Browning Machine Gun) round which was developed after the U.S. Army captured one of the World War I-vintage German T-Gewehr antitank rifles and used it as a test gun to perfect a similar American round. Once the round had been created, it was coupled with John Moses Browning's new machine gun and adopted by the U.S. Army in 1921.

During this same period, Julian Hatcher suggested the .50 BMG round be used for a sniper rifle as well. While a few feeble attempts were made to create a long-range sniper rifle during World War II and again during the Korean War, the lack of a quality optical system and good muzzle brakes (as well as lack of interest by the U.S. military) meant that it would still be several years before anyone started doing serious work on the concept.

One solution to the occasional need for a long-range sniping weapon which dates back to World War II (and perhaps World War I) is to use a machine gun as a quasi-sniper rifle. Toward this end, optical sights or night-vision equipment have been used on machine guns stationed in areas where enemy activity is expected. Such use, though, has not been entirely successful, since machine guns lack the precision of sniper rifles, and the size of the machine gun and the need for a crew to serve it makes the gunners more easily detectable. (Also, the burst needed to saturate an area in order to hit a target can hardly be considered in the same light as the single, accurate shot of most sniper rifles.) Thus, the machine gun has proven to be less than satisfactory for general use as a long-range sniper weapon.

Interest in long-range sniping continued in small

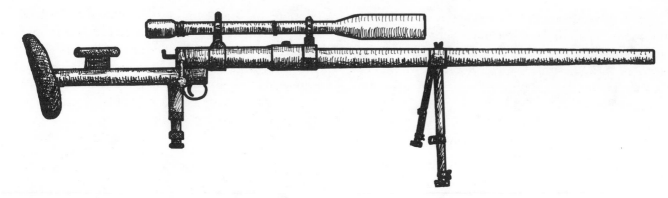

The single-shot Horstkamp is based on the old Sharps rifle, with a dropping block action. The "Sniper" is made of stainless steel and has a wooden, Monte Carlo stock.

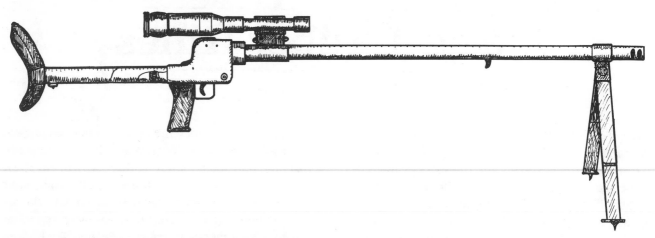

In the early 1950s, Lt. Col. William Brophy converted a captured PTRD to the .50 BMG, which proved that such a "super" sniper rifle was both accurate and practical.

circles within the U.S. military, with some excellent research being done by Captain William Brophy (using the Soviet PTRD rebarreled to .50-caliber) and Lt. Col. Frank Conway (using a modified German PzB39 with a .50-caliber barrel). However, it was not until the Vietnam War that optical systems finally became good enough so that U.S. snipers in the field could report seeing targets of opportunity outside even the extreme range of 1,000 to 1,500 yards of their 7.62mm NATO rifles.

With these realizations came renewed interest in large-caliber sniper rifles capable of reaching out to 2,000 yards or more. Studies done by the military proved that the .50-caliber BMG round was suitable for such use, and it has become more or less the standard for large-caliber sniper rifles. (This is also the largest caliber United States citizens can own without special permits from the Bureau of Alcohol, Tobacco and Firearms, making it the upper limit for manufacturers wishing to cater to sport shooters as well as the military/police market.)

There are currently two methods used to develop new, large-caliber sniper rifles. One is to base the weapon's design on the heavy actions of World War I-vintage anti-tank rifles. Weapons most often used for this are the German 13mm T-Gewehr (Tank Gun) and the Boys Mark I and Mark II. While the thick armor of World War II tanks made these rifles obsolete for fighting tanks, new optical systems and muzzle brakes make it possible to use the weapons as the basis of new long-range sniper rifles.

The other route is to create a whole new, large-caliber sniper rifle. More and more of these guns are coming into the marketplace, since, as the concept gains popularity, firearms designers are only too happy to have another type of weapon on which to exercise their creative talents. (It should be noted that even here, there is frequent borrowing from the past; for example, the .50-caliber machine gun barrel often serves as the basis around which new rifle designs are created.)

Creativity is also being exercised in the design

of new muzzle brakes to tame the recoil of these weapons. This offers a big improvement to those interested in using such weapons—while military leaders of the past discovered that those volunteering to fire the heavy-recoiling tank guns were few and far between (the recoil was in the range of fifty foot pounds!), the same weapon used for sniping now enjoys a much milder recoil, thanks to new muzzle brake designs.

Ammunition is another area which requires new designs and expertise. Because machine-gun rounds are ideally a "little off" in order to aid dispersal during automatic fire, much manufactured ammunition is not loaded to obtain the round's full accuracy potential. Therefore, the creation of ammunition which will enjoy the full inherent accuracy of the new rifles is another area needing skill and thought.

(Currently, many users of sniper rifles reload their own ammunition, since accurate rounds are not readily available, especially to nonmilitary users. Those embarking on such a course must take great care when reloading ammunition since a high primer can cause premature ignition; with shells as powerful as the .50 BMG, this translates into a shower of deadly shrapnel from the cartridge case. Also, bolts on bolt-action rifles which are not yet locked into place can be propelled out of the back of the rifle with—as in one actual case—enough force to blow clear through the body of the unfortunate accident victim. Shooters with these large rifles should be very cautious with reloads and always wear proper eye protection.)

Will the large-caliber sniper rifles survive the test of time or will they just be another strange development that leads to a dead end in the evolution of small arms? Only time can tell, and there are a lot of unknowns in the equation. New considerations include the limited mobility of a sniper with one of these heavy rifles and—for the military—the logistical problem of supplying yet another type of ammunition.

There are also many technical points not yet fully explored. How often will a sniper find a location from which he can find enemy targets beyond 1,000 yards? How quickly will the enemy be able to locate a sniper firing from over 1,000 yards, given the fact that few points in most terrains offer a vantage point of more than one thousand yards? Can human targets even be hit, given the fact that the bullet's in-flight time is 3.75 seconds for targets at 2,000 yards (which translates to leads of ten to fifteen yards

or more for a moving target)? Will the .50 BMG bullet penetrate too much material for use in most urban environments by police or antiterrorist teams? The answer to any of these questions might lead to the conclusion that the large-caliber sniper rifle is not really as practical as military and police decision-makers might hope.

On the flip side of things, the sniper of tomorrow will be moderately mobile, able to engage larger targets over a mile away, and, with a bullet costing only a few dollars, destroy a million-dollar airplane, ignite fuel storage tanks, disable SAM (Surface-to-Air Missile) sites, trash radar dishes, or ruin vital communications equipment.

The idea of such a soldier must certainly be appealing to many would-be military purchasers and tacticians and a nightmare to those guarding complexes containing valuable military personnel and equipment.

Conversely, for those defending a base or a ship, the large .50-caliber sniper rifle has proven to be effective in exploding cluster bomblets, aircraft-dispersed mines (designed to render an airfield unusable), and mines floating in the water—all jobs beyond the abilities of .30-caliber sniper rifles. Again, one sniper can destroy thousands of dollars worth of military hardware for just a few dollars a shot—and still be ready to engage enemy troops or vehicles if the need should arise.

Currently, most of the work on this type of rifle is seemingly being done solely by the United States. No other countries are known to be working on large-caliber sniper rifles even though the .50 BMG or its Soviet counterpart, the 12.7x108mm DShK round, are readily available in most parts of the world.

At any rate, it would seem probable that at least a few of these weapons will be developed and tested—officially or unofficially—on battlefields around the world in the very near future. Following such use, the rifle will either become another tool in the arsenals of various armies worldwide or sink into oblivion for all except a few hobby shooting enthusiasts.

Aimstar/1500 and Daisy 600

Little information is currently available on the Aimstar. The rifle was originally designed by RAI (Research Armanent Industries) of Jacksonville, Arkansas, and was subsequently manufactured and marketed by Iver Johnson's Arms as the Browning Model 1500 Special Application. Because Iver

The 23-pound Daisy 600 breaks down into lighter parts for easy carrying. The rifle has a fluted barrel and an adjustable stock. The receiver will accept most optical scopes as well as night-vision equipment. Photo courtesy of Daisy Manufacturing Company.

Johnson's Arms recently went bankrupt and then reorganized, and since the company apparently wants to sell the rifles only to select buyers, one has to suspect that the Aimstar has not enjoyed the publicity or marketing that is needed to make such a rifle a commercial success.

The single-shot, bolt-action rifle lacks a fore grip, and a tube projects from the lower receiver to form the bipod mount. The fluted barrel is free-floated and totally exposed; a large muzzle brake (called an "accumulator" in company literature) is attached to help tame recoil. A pistol grip is used with the stock, and is connected to the base of the grip and to the rear of the receiver. The butt of the stock is adjustable, as is the cheek piece.

The scope base of the 1500 has a ranging system which the company claims makes it possible to adjust for bullet drop in one-hundred-meter increments from 300 to 1,500 meters regardless of the scope mounted on the rifle.

During the late 1980s, Daisy (the same company that sells air rifles) started marketing the Aimstar 1500 as their Model 600. The Model 600 is available in 14.5mm, 12.7x108mm, and .50 BMG chamberings.

Barrett Model 82/82A1

The Barrett 82 is one of the new breed of "heavy rifles" designed to carry out a number of tasks in addition to long-range sniping. When used in the sniper mode, it becomes the only known semiauto .50-caliber sniper rifle in production. As such, the Barrett would seem to be a frontline contender for many police and military applications requiring a heavy .50-caliber rifle. (The fact that its operating controls, such as the safety and trigger, "feel" like an AR-15/M16 rifle can't hurt its chances either, since this would minimize training procedures for those who have adopted the AR-15 family of rifles.)

The rifle was developed by Ronnie G. Barrett and a team which included the well-known designer Steve Blair, who perfected the DTA Mil/Brake. The Barrett 82 semiauto action is capable of firing a quick second shot should it be needed, thanks to a large-capacity, detachable box magazine holding 11 rounds (as opposed to the single-shot style of most other large-caliber sniping rifles). The rifle also enjoys more modern lines than most other bolt-action style large-caliber rifles (modern lines which have undoubtedly helped get it into a number of magazine spreads, and even into the sci-fi movie *Robocop*, where it was used to "hunt down" the character in the title role).

The Barrett 82 operates with a delayed blowback system, with the bolt and barrel recoiling backward together a short distance before the rotating bolt (with three locking lugs) unlocks. At that point, the bolt continues back to eject a spent case, then cycles forward to strip off another shell from the magazine and chamber it. While the delayed blowback system is not noted for absorbing recoil, the Barrett 82 also has a well-designed muzzle brake and a rubber butt plate which make the rifle quite comfortable to shoot.

The Barrett 82 design also makes it easy to clean and maintain. It is easily broken down by pulling two pins out of the rifle; this allows the upper and lower assemblies to be separated, exposing the bolt carrier/bolt and recoil spring/buffer as well as the

Prototype (serial number 2) of the Barrett Model 82. Unlike the 82A1, this model lacks an internal accelerator system and the bolt is rotated purely by the inertia of the bolt carrier when the barrel comes up against its stop. Rifle shown here is mounted on the U.S. M122 tripod. Photo courtesy of Barrett Firearms Manufacturing, Inc.

Prototype of the original Barrett Model 82. The internal operation of the rifle was different from the current models and the barrel was fastened to the lower receiver rather than the upper cover. Unlike subsequent models, which are striker fired, this model had an internal hammer. Photo courtesy of Barrett Firearms Manufacturing, Inc.

trigger group in the lower half of the rifle. The upper half consists of the buffer cover, four barrel recoil springs, the barrel, scope base, and upper receiver, which stays in one unit.

The scope base consists of a one-piece dovetail which is bolted to the top of the receiver. The unit will accept most scopes and can be adapted to others with a base plate.

The upper receiver has a scope block permanently attached to it, while the lower receiver comes

with a bipod. As a multifunction rifle capable of being used against APCs or the like, the Barrett 82 also can be fitted into the M60 GPMG (General Purpose Machine Gun) mount or the M122 tripod mount to function in capacities other than that of sniper rifle (an important consideration for military buyers).

The body of the Barrett 82 is made of steel stampings with a gray parkerized finish (an optional black Teflon finish is available). The rifle uses a

The Barrett LSW, which was the prototype for the Model 82A1. Rings just below the carrying handle and at the upper half of the butt plate are connected to the disassembly pins. Note the new style "rounded" muzzle brake found on this model. Photo courtesy of Barrett Firearms Manufacturing, Inc.

The Barrett 82A1 can be field-stripped for maintenance in just a few seconds. The scope block is mounted directly to the cover to assure its zero following reassembly. Photo courtesy of Barrett Firearms Manufacturing, Inc.

The Barrett 82A1 differs from previous models of Barrett rifles in that it has iron sights, a more efficient muzzle brake, and a lighter trigger pull. Photo courtesy of Barrett Firearms Manufacturing, Inc.

1-in-15 barrel twist, which is best suited to most military ammunition, making the rifle capable of using special-purpose .50 BMG military ammunition as well as other rounds which may be developed for the .50-caliber machine gun in the near future.

The Barrett borrows heavily from the quality designs of other firearms in use worldwide (which makes good sense both from a production standpoint as well as in parts replacement and repair work). Thus, the trigger group contains the familiar AR-15 trigger, safety, pistol grip, and trigger spring, while the bolt assembly has the Browning M2 machine-gun sear, firing pin, and (modified) charging lever. Those familiar with the U.S. M60 machine gun will also recognize that its bipod is used on the Barrett 82.

The Barrett 82 has gone through several design changes. The original rifle had a solid steel receiver and a one-inch diameter barrel. The new 82A1 has a fluted barrel with a hard chrome-plated chamber to minimize extracting problems over extended use. A carrying handle is also available for the new version, as are iron sights (the latter two features are ideal when the rifle is used in its Light Support Weapon [LSW] role).

It would appear that the Barrett 82 is the front-runner in the large-caliber sniper rifle race, since it can be used in a number of heavy rifle roles in addition to sniping. The AR-15-style feel and the ability to deliver rapid fire if needed are additional advantages of this rifle.

Boys Mark 1/Mark 2 Anti-Tank Rifle

This .55-caliber weapon was created in the 1930s and was named after its principal designer, Captain Boys, following his death. The rifle has a bolt action with a top-mounted, detachable magazine. The barrel and breech of the Boys rifle recoils along a rail upon firing. This action, coupled with a heavily padded butt plate, muzzle brake, and monopod, helps to tame recoil a bit (though the weapon is still noted as being a beast to shoot).

As early as World War II, various groups in and out of the U.S. military have tried their hand at adding a scope to this rifle and rebarreling it for the .50 BMG round. The results, though, were not often encouraging, and the recoil was still excessive. There is no known instance of this weapon being used as a sniper rifle in combat.

The Boys 55 continues to be used as the basis

for testing sniper rifle ideas and, with new muzzle brakes available, its basic design may yet see development for actual use as a sniper weapon.

Browning M2-HB

This version of the Browning Machine Gun was actually modified for semiauto fire and equipped with the U.S. military's periscope sight, developed for the machine gun; it also featured a short bipod and a shoulder pad with a monopod attached to it. The result was a weapon that was too big and clumsy to be of any use anywhere! There is no known use of this weapon as a sniper rifle in the semiauto mode.

Unmodified Browning M2-HB machine guns with scopes were also occasionally deployed in a sniper-like capacity, though such use still required a crew to operate the gun, and it was far from mobile or overly accurate beyond 1,500 yards (ideal for large targets but not for individual troops). Thus, the M2-HB was not really a "sniper rifle" as such.

Horstkamp Target and SWAT Rifles

These .50-caliber rifles are designed and built by Klaus Horstkamp, owner of State Arms in Waunakee, Wisconsin. The rifles are made on a more-or-less custom basis and are currently marketed by Stroessner & Hunting Firearms. The basic design is based on the Mauser, so that the weapon is similar to the old German T-Gewehr. Barrel length is in accordance with the customer's wishes (36-inch barrels are recommended).

There are several versions of the rifle available. The Target Version has stocks which are usually made of camouflaged fiberglass; wood stocks are optional, along with stainless-steel bolts or a blued finish. The trigger pull is adjustable, and the top of the receiver is drilled and tapped for scope mounting. An offset Monte Carlo thumbhole stock

is used so that the scope can be mounted on the side of the receiver; a left-handed version of the rifle is also available). The parkerized rifles come equipped with a Harris bipod and a heavy muzzle brake.

The SWAT Version of the Horstkamp rifle is similar to the Target Version, except it uses a shorter receiver (with the bolt being removed to reload the rifle) than the Horstkamp. The SWAT rifle's weight is also considerably lighter than some versions of the Target.

Horstkamp offers bronze bullets, which are recommended for use with the rifles for best accuracy (the Horstkamp barrels use a 1-in-9 1/2 twist as opposed to the military 1-in-15 twist for the .50 BMG bullet). One MOA accuracy beyond 1,000 yards is generally possible given good ammunition and lack of crosswinds. The company also offers reloading presses for the .50 BMG cartridge, as well as heavy silencers for use with special heavy bullets. The Horstkamp muzzle brakes are among the most effective in reducing recoil, making these rifles relatively comfortable to shoot.

Horstkamp Sniper Rifle

Also marketed by Stroessner & Hunting Firearms, this single-shot Horstkamp rifle is based on the old Sharps rifle with a dropping block action. The Sniper model is made of stainless steel and has a wooden, Monte Carlo stock with sporter rifle lines to it (the purchaser has a choice of walnut or maple stock). The top is drilled and tapped for scope mounting (with the scope mounted directly over the barrel), and iron sights and a Harris bipod are also included. The Sniper's muzzle brake has slots (rather than the holes found on other Horstkamp rifles) and has a tang safety. The rifle comes with German double-set triggers.

Horstkamp also has a bullpup model of this rifle,

The single-shot, anti-armor PzB39 rifle with a new .50-caliber barrel attached by Lt. Col. Frank Conway demonstrated that the idea of a long-range sniper rifle was practical.

designated the VMP T80E1. With cartridges this powerful, it is doubtful that a bullpup design will catch on, since a cartridge which is too hot might conceivably blow up, thereby injuring the shooter's face. While such occurrences are very rare (and certainly do not reflect on the quality of the Horstkamp or any other rifle), the power of the .50 caliber round makes such an incident much more serious than when dealing with smaller caliber rifles.

The Horstkamp Sniper is said to have been used by a U.S. Navy SEAL team during the Grenada invasion, and 800-yard, one-shot kills are reportedly made with it.

Mauser T-Gewehr

The German T-Gewehr (Tank Gun) was developed in 1919 in an effort to defeat tanks. The single-shot rifle is, for all practical purposes, an enlarged Mauser bolt-action rifle with a heavy bipod mounted at its front and a pistol grip added to the stock behind the trigger. The 13mm cartridge and long barrel developed enough bullet velocity to work well, but improvements in armor soon made the heavy rifle obsolete.

The rifle's action has served as the test vehicle in various countries for many experiments to create a sniper rifle. Quite often, the rifle is rebarreled for the .50 BMG round which seems to be the most readily suited for long-range sniper use.

While the original T-Gewehr lines are seen in modern sniper rifles, the basic design is still being used, and this rifle has greatly influenced the development of such weapons.

McMillan M87 ELR

Gale McMillan has produced custom-stocked, super-accurate rifles and fiberglass stocks for several decades, having helped design the stock for the U.S. Marines' M40A1 sniper rifle.

In mid-1987, McMillan introduced his bolt-action rifle to the general public; the rifle is said to have been designed at the request of the U.S. Navy, although no information is available as to whether or not rifles have actually been purchased for military use.

The M87 has a fiberglass stock, adjustable trigger pull (from two to four pounds) and a matte black finish on its metal parts. Its major deviation from the bolt-action rifles covered in this chapter comes in McMillan's use of a massive recoil brake (apparently a modified tank cannon design), which makes it possible to keep the rifle's weight far less than that of other large-caliber guns. The M87, which can be broken down into two parts with a maximum length of 39 inches, is considerably easier to transport than most other large sniper rifles. The M87 is currently offered with the Leupold 20x Ultra M1 scope.

PTRD Antitank Rifle

The 14.5mm PTRD (Protivotankovoe Ruzh'yo obr) was developed by the Soviets in the late 1930s and early 1940s. The heavy round developed for it was later used as a machine-gun round when the PTRD proved to be obsolete in combating the heavy armor developed for modern German tanks.

The PTRD is a single-shot weapon. Rounds are loaded into its bolt-action through a large slot on the top of the receiver when the bolt is retracted.

During the early 1950s, the PTRD served as a test vehicle for U.S. research into the possibilities of long-range sniper rifles. This research came about when a decorated sniper during the Korean War, Lt. Col. William Brophy, returned to the States and converted a captured PTRD into a .50 BMG to create a "super sniper" rifle. This rifle, fitted with a 20x power Unertl scope, apparently saw limited use in Korea and is said to have scored hits on communist soldiers at 1,000 to 2,000 yards. When Brophy returned to the U.S., the U.S. Army allowed him to use this rifle, as well as others, in a series of tests which compared his .50 caliber weapon with the standard .30-06 sniper rifle.

Brophy found that the .50-caliber PTRD could scope hits at 1,000 yards almost 50 percent of the time, while the Army's sniper rifle did only a bit better than 10 percent. (Brophy was limited to issued .50-caliber machine-gun ammunition which was not as accurate as it might have been; to have such a high number of hits at 1,000 yards shows the merit of a large-caliber sniper rifle.)

Despite the success of his work, nothing was done by the U.S. military following the publication of his final report in 1955. There is no known use of this weapon as a sniper rifle by the USSR.

PzB39

The PzB38 (Panzerbuchse Modell 1938) was created by the German Army as an anti-armor weapon. As such, the rifle was both too hard to manufacture and too ineffective, thanks to the ever-increasing thicknesses of armor being encountered on the battlefields of World War II. The Germans later tried simplifying the semiauto action to a manual action, denoting it as their PzB39.

While the single-shot PzB39 rifle still proved to be ineffective as an anti-armor weapon, it was to later serve as a test vehicle for .50-caliber sniper experiments in the United States during the mid-1940s. It was then that Lt. Col. Frank B. Conway attached a .50 BMG barrel to the rifle, along with a double-baffle muzzle brake and a 3-8x power variable scope (also "borrowed" from the German Army). Conway's modified PzB was eventually tested in the field in Vietnam as a sniper rifle (fitted with a 3-9x ART scope); however, the United States' involvement in the war was curtailed before it was actually used. While little became of Conway's work, it nonetheless demonstrated the practicality of a long-range sniper rifle.

Specifications Large-Caliber Sniper Rifles

Name	Barrel Length (in.)	Weight Unloaded (lbs.)	Length (in.)	Magazine Capacity
Aimstar 600 (Daisy)	29	23	53	0
Aimstar 1500	33	30	57	0
Barrett 82	37	35	66	11
Barrett 82A1	33	32.5	61	11
Barrett LSW	33	32.5	61	11
Boys Mark 1/ Mark 2[1]	36	36	63.5	5
Horstkamp Target	36[2]	30-58	64	0
Horstkamp SWAT	36[2]	20-27	64	0
Horstkamp Sniper	36[2]	22-32	64	0
Mauser T-Gewehr[1]	38.69	39	66.13	0
McMillan M87	29	21	53	0
PTRD[1]	48.3	38.12	78.7	0
PzB39[1]	42.75	27.25	62.25	0

[1] Specifications given in the table are of the original firearms; when these firearms are employed as experimental test weapons, the specifications were probably different than those shown.
[2] Other barrel lengths are available.

7

.22 LR Sniper and Practice Rifles

While the .22 LR (as well as such related rimfire cartridges as the .22 Short and .22 Long) doesn't have the power necessary for most sniper purposes, the rounds *can* be silenced very efficiently. The .22 LR is also ideal for practice where shooting ranges for centerfire rifles aren't available or are too far away to make daily practice convenient. (In fact, with the use of low-noise CCI CB Longs or Federal CB Long Caps, a .22 rifle can be used for practice indoors or in urban backyard areas. Shooters should, however, be sure to check local ordinances.)

There are a number of .22 rifles on the market. Listed below are some .22s which are ideal from a dependability or accuracy standpoint, as well as several "custom" style rifles equipped with integral silencers. (It should be noted that silencers are also available from several companies. Often, purchasing a sporting .22 rifle and adding a silencer is a much less expensive way to obtain a silenced weapon as opposed to purchasing one of the complete rifle packages with an integral silencer.)

All the semiauto .22 rifles listed here are reliable given *quality* ammunition. If bargain-basement ammunition of dubious origin is used, the guns may have an occasional failure in chambering or ejection.

A few of these .22 rifles (like the Ruger 77/22 and the Jäger AP-74) very nearly duplicate the handling characteristics of the larger rifles they are modeled after, making them ideal for practice. (For more information on the centerfire counterparts

to these rifles, see Chapter 4 for bolt-action guns and Chapter 5 for semiauto designs.)

When practicing with a .22 rifle as a substitute for a larger centerfire rifle, it is important that the scope and rifle approximate the larger rifle as closely as possible. Toward this end, adding weights to the .22 to make it as heavy as the centerfire, having a scope with the same style of reticle, and having the safety, trigger pull, and basic operation as similar as possible all are important. While it is nearly impossible to create an identical .22 rifle copy of centerfire sniper rifles, it is possible to create a close approximation which will be a great practice aid and which will enable a sniper to cheaply and conveniently hone his marksmanship skills.

The scopes available for .22 rifles are generally quite poor. One good alternative to the three-quarter-inch .22 scope is to use adapter rings (readily available from most gunsmiths or in a gun store) which allow the use of one-inch scopes on rimfire mounts. This will enable a shooter to use a quality scope, since even inexpensive one-inch scopes are generally far superior to most .22 scopes.

For those who use a specialized scope with a post, dot, or similar reticle not readily available in the "low end" of the price scale, purchasing a second scope for a .22 can be an expensive proposition. One very inexpensive alternative is the Daisy Point Sight 800, which costs very little and allows the user to easily choose from a number of different reticle inserts. (More about this scope

A .22 adapter kit (shown next to the detached magazines) allows practice with inexpensive .22 LR rounds. The SGW AR-15 (top) has a twenty-four-inch barrel, a Tasco scope, Harris bipod, Choate E2 stock, and DTA Mil/Brake. The center rifle is a Colt Carbine. Shown at bottom is the SGW barrel/receiver assembly, which allows one to convert a sniper rifle into a standard one.

and others in the next chapter.)

A few rifles, including the HK-91 series, AR-15/ M16 series, and Mini-14, also have .22 adapter kits available. While accuracy from most of these adapters is not quite as good as that of a .22 rifle and the point of impact changes when switching from .22 to centerfire use, the kits do allow shooting from the actual weapon that will be used for sniping. These kits are generally a bit more expensive than many .22 rifles, and care should be taken not to let lead build up in the barrel (using copper-washed .22 LR bullets or shooting a few copper-jacketed centerfire bullets down the barrel from time to time will prevent this problem). If lead bullets are used in a semiauto rifle, care should also be taken to check the gas port to be sure lead shavings aren't building up there.

The cost of an adapter kit or a .22 practice rifle will soon pay for itself after shooting off several hundred rounds of ammunition with .22 LR cartridges (given the high cost of centerfire rounds).

Beretta Super Sport X and Olimpia X

Beretta currently offers two .22 rifles which have a unique design, allowing them to be fired as bolt-action rifles or as semiautos, depending on how the bolt handle is positioned. The Olimpia X has a heavy barrel and special Diopter iron sights, while the Super Sport X has standard sporter sights. Both rifles have receivers which are drilled and tapped for the company's 3-7x 20 scopes.

The lines of the stocks are nearly identical to the Beretta 500/501/502 series, making the rifles ideal training/practice companions to the centerfire guns. The stocks are made of walnut with an oiled nonglare finish; checkering is also found on the grip and fore grip. The metal on the Super Sport X is blued, while the Olimpia X has a tough nonglare black finish. Both models come with a black rubber recoil pad and have chromed bolts. The bolt handle is well ahead of the normal position on most bolt-action rifles, which may take a bit of getting used to for those accustomed to standard rifles.

F.I.E. GR-8 Black Beauty

The GR-8, imported into the United States by F.I.E., is a Brazilian-made copy of the semiauto Remington Nylon 66 except for its lower price tag.

The rifle's light weight makes it ideal for use as a sniping rifle, but it may make it less than ideal for those who substitute it for a heavy sniper rifle during practice. The rifle's tough action demands minimal maintenance but, should repair be needed, the rifle must be taken to a gunsmith, as attempts to disassemble and reassemble the rifle are not jobs an amateur gunsmith should undertake.

The rifle has a 14-round tubular magazine located in the stock, and the rounds feed forward to the receiver; double extractors make for sure extraction with this rifle. The GR-8 has a tang safety with scope mount cuts on its receiver, as well as having iron sights.

F.I.E. Model 122

The bolt-action Model 122 is made in Brazil and is imported into the United States by F.I.E. It has a hardwood Monte Carlo stock and a detachable box magazine. The receiver is dovetailed for scope mounting and has adjustable iron sights as well. The slide safety is located at the upper left side of the receiver behind the bolt, and the rifle also has a red cocking indicator. The low price tag on this rifle makes it a good buy as a practice gun.

Field Arms Mark 3

Made for actual use as a sniper rifle, the bolt-action Mark 3 is similar to the Field Arms Mark 1, except that it is chambered for the .22 LR. The Mark 3's integral silencer does an excellent job of quieting the report of the .22 so that shots are made with very little disturbance.

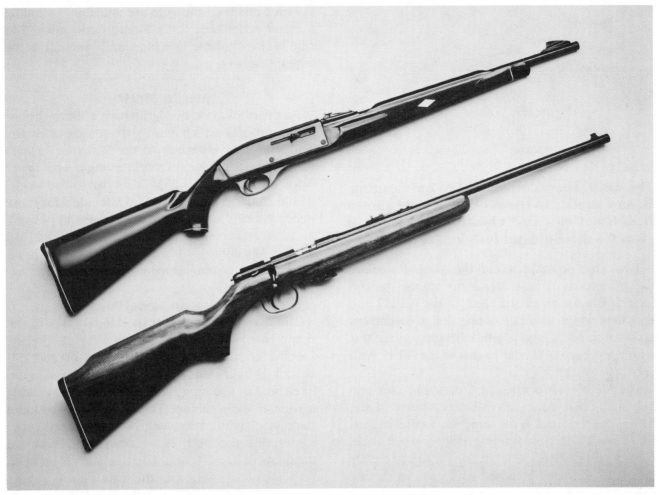

The F.I.E. Black Beauty GR-8 (top) and Model 122 (bottom), excellent .22 rifles, carry a low price tag, making them good buys for those needing a .22 for practice or sniping. Photo courtesy of F.I.E.

Jäger AP-74

The Italian-made AP-74, currently being imported into the United States by EMF, looks and feels much like an AR-15. Several hundred rounds of shooting may be needed to break in this rifle and to clean the bits of metal chips (apparently left behind when the receiver is milled out) out of the rifle's action. This, and careful lubrication with Break-Free CLP and the use of good ammunition, should keep the rifle functioning very reliably, giving the shooter a lot of practice at a low cost.

The rifle comes out of the box with an A1-style fore grip, which can easily be replaced. Take off the front sight assembly, which is held in place by four hex screws with one pair over the second, and unscrew the flash hider, removing the AP-74's fore grip halves and handguard spring. Slide an AR-15 handguard ring (readily available from suppliers like SGW) over the barrel and then over the old handguard ring, and place a set of A2 stocks (SGW,

again) in place, and then replace the front scope mount and flash hider back on the rifle. Some fitting is required to get the front of the handguards to go into the front sight base, but this is easily done with a wood rasp or file on the plastic handguard. A small shim cut from a plastic bottle placed between the original AP-74 handguard ring and the new AR-15 ring will tighten everything up. Total cost for this modification: a little elbow grease and about $28, for a rifle which handles identically to the AR-15 A2. (Adding some weights inside the handguard will also bring the rifle up to the correct weight. Wire, tightly wrapped around the barrel, or lead weights glued to the inside of the handguard are ideal for this.)

Unfortunately, the dimensions and most parts of the AP-74 are quite different from those of the AR-15. However, the rifle does accept AR-15 scope-mount systems, as well as laser mounts or similar devices which fit into the rifle's bayonet mount.

The AP-74, shown broken down for cleaning, is very similar to the AR-15. The rifle shown here has a modified Choate E2 stock which gives it a three-quarter inch longer pull.

Two other departures from the AR-15 design are the placement of the magazine release button (which is a lot lower than that of the AR-15) and the safety, which is of a cross-bolt design on current production rifles. A good gunsmith can replace this with a lever safety similar to that of the AR-15 with very little work.

The AP-74's rear peep sight, flash suppressor, and bolt hold-open device are all very similar to the AR-15, and the stock is the same size as the original AR-15 stock. For those wanting a longer stock, E&L's rubber butt plate is the quickest way to add a little length to the rifle. Standard AR-15 stocks can be made to fit the AP-74 by reworking with a rasp or file and a sharp knife.

Several AP-74 models are available, including a commando version with a wire stock and wooden stock models (such a version is not as ideal for practice purposes as the standard AP-74). A .32 ACP version is also available; it might have some actual sniper applications for those looking for a bit more power than is offered by the .22 LR while still staying well below the power of the .223. Interestingly, the .32 ACP picks up some extra velocity in the AP-74 barrel, making the round a bit more powerful when fired from the carbine. (Magazine capacity of the .32 ACP version is 15 rounds).

For those using some version of the AR-15 as their major sniping rifle, the AP-74 makes an ideal practice gun.

Kimber Model 82B

Kimber's bolt-action Model 82 is nearly identical to the centerfire Model 84 except for its .22 LR chambering. This makes it perfect for those who choose the Kimber 84 for their sniper rifle and need a .22 rifle for use in practice.

Three styles of the rifle are available, including a classic-style stock and a Monte Carlo stock. The rifle is also available in a high-grade version as the Super American.

Marlin 25/25M

All the rifles made by Marlin have a Micro-Groove rifling process which makes them very accurate. The Marlin 25 is similar to the 780 (see below) except for its hardwood stock, giving it a bit lower price tag. The Marlin 25M is similar to the Model 25 but chambered for the .22 WMR (ideal for those needing a rifle with a bit more range and power). A takedown version of the .22 WMR rifle, the 25MB Midget Magnum, is also available; this rifle has a barrel which is removable for compact storage.

Marlin Model 70

The hardwood stock on the Model 70 is of the "plain-Jane" style, devoid of expensive checkering (such a stock is also found on Models 60 and 75C described below). It is a good buy for those more interested in shooting rimfire rifles than in looking at them in a gun cabinet. The Model 70 has a Monte Carlo stock with a receiver grooved for scope rings; sometimes the rifle is also available with an inexpensive Tasco scope. The rear sight is an open buckhorn ramp sight, and the front sight is a ramp blade. A variation of this rifle, the 70P Papoose, is also available. It has a shorter fore grip and a short barrel, which can be unscrewed from the rifle for compact storage.

The safeties on the Marlin semiautos are located behind the triggers (as is the case with most Remington guns), and the bolt handle can be depressed to lock the bolt open for cleaning.

Ram-Line offers a pistol grip, glass-filled, all-plastic folding stock for the Model 70 (similar to that for the 10/22 and Mini-14) which might be of interest to those looking for a pistol grip practice .22. The cost is approximately $68.

Marlin Models 60/75C/990

Models 60, 75C, and 990 use tubular magazines but are otherwise very similar to the Model 70. The tubular magazine is fine for practice, but is a bit awkward to reload, making the Model 70 a better choice for those wanting to use the rifle for actual sniper purposes.

Unlike the Model 70, Marlin's tubular magazine semiauto rifles have a hold-open device which locks the bolt open after the last round has been fired.

The Marlin 60 rifle has the accuracy of other Marlin rifles coupled with a low price tag. This is a longer version of the Model 75C Carbine. Photo courtesy of Marlin.

The Marlin 75C shown here is often available at discount stores and makes an excellent .22 for practice shooting. Photo courtesy of Marlin.

Chambered for the .22 WMR, the Marlin 782 has a detachable box magazine and a walnut Monte Carlo stock. Photo courtesy of Marlin.

With a long tube magazine under its barrel and chambering for the .22 WMR, the Marlin 783 has a bit more power than the standard .22 LR. Photo courtesy of Marlin.

The 60 and 75C are often available on sale at discount stores; their low price tags make them excellent buys for those interested in obtaining a .22 rifle for very little money. The Model 60 is the rifle version, while the Model 75C is the carbine version, having a shorter barrel and magazine. The 990 is nearly identical to the 60, but has a higher quality finish overall with a checkered walnut stock.

Marlin 780/782

This bolt-action rifle has a detachable box magazine and a walnut Monte Carlo stock. The safety is located just behind the bolt lever and the upper receiver is grooved for scope mounts. The iron sights are adjustable, and the grooved upper receiver reduces glare when iron sights are used. Like other Marlin rifles, the micro-groove rifling makes this a nice practice rifle. A nearly identical model, the 782, is available in .22 WMR.

Marlin 781/783

The Marlin 781 is similar to the 780 except for its tubular magazine, which is located under the barrel. A similar rifle, the 783, is also marketed by

Marlin, though the 783 is chambered for .22 WMR, giving it a bit more power and range. As with other Marlin rifles, either of these would make an ideal practice rifle, and could even be pressed into service should a .22 rifle be used as a sniper weapon.

Mitchell Arms AK-22/Galil 22

Mitchell Arms is currently importing Italian-made .22 versions of the AK-47 and Galil rifles in both .22 LR and .22 Magnum. Although the weight of these rifles is only about half that of their centerfire counterparts, the basic handling characteristics are nearly identical to the larger guns, making them potential practice rifles for those who adopt sniper rifles based on the AK-47/Dragunov or Galil guns.

Ruger 10/22

The Sturm, Ruger 10/22 is one of the most popular .22 rifles in the United States. It is highly reliable and accurate, and has a wealth of accessories available for it. As a result, it is the first choice for many looking for a semiauto .22 rifle. The 10/22 operates well with a wide range of ammunition and seems to need fewer repairs than most other .22 rifles. Two basic versions of the rifle are readily available: the Carbine, which has a saddle-rifle-style carbine stock (available in both birch and walnut) with a front barrel band, and the Sporter, which has a straight butt plate, sporter-style walnut stock with checkering.

The Ruger 10/22 can be easily disassembled by simply removing the screw in the stock (along with the barrel band on the carbine version); this frees the barrel and receiver for removal from the stock. Drifting out two bolts in the receiver frees the trigger group, and the bolt assembly is easily removed The 10/22 is easy to maintain and clean.

The 10/22 comes with a scope mount and mounting screws which can be placed on the receiver. The cross-bolt safety is located in front of the trigger guard; this makes it unlike many other guns, though it still has a bit of the feel of the

Known for its reliability and accuracy, the Ruger 10/22 is one of the most popular .22s in the States. Shown is the Sporter version. Photo courtesy of Sturm, Ruger & Company.

The 10/22 Standard Carbine has a barrel band and a saddle rifle-style butt plate. The rifle is noted for its reliability, and there is a wealth of accessories available for this carbine. Photo courtesy of Sturm, Ruger & Company.

An excellent .22 bolt-action sniper or practice rifle, the 77/22 comes with iron sights and one-inch rings capable of using quality scopes. Photo courtesy of Sturm, Ruger & Company.

A 77/22 with the Z stock gives the rifle an attractive and effective camouflage finish. The laminated stock is comprised of highly moisture-resistant layers of brown- and green-dyed wood. Photo courtesy of Sturm, Ruger & Company.

Garand/M14-style rifles. (A good gunsmith could change the safety to the actual M14 style if it were really needed.)

A bolt hold-open lever is in front of the trigger guard, and the magazine release is on the lower side of the receiver in front of the trigger guard. For those who would like a Garand/Mini-14-style magazine release, Ram-Line offers a "no gunsmithing" extended release for about $4. The 10/22 has a rotary magazine which allows 10 rounds; excellent Ram-Line banana magazines are also available which hold 30 or 50 rounds.

Many companies carry aftermarket accessories for the 10/22, so that it can be modified for nearly all tastes and styles of shooting.

Ruger 77/10

The Ruger 77/22 rifle is chambered for .22 LR and might be suited for some types of sniper use. It is certainly ideal as a practice rifle for those who use the centerfire Ruger 77 as a sniper rifle, since the stock and weight of the 77/22 are quite close to the 77.

The 77/10 comes with one-inch scope rings, so that the same type of scope which is used on the 77 might be used on the 77/22. The 77/22 uses the 10-round magazine of the 10/22 and will also accept the extended Ramline 30- and 50-round magazines. The rifle has a three-position safety.

Several versions of the 77/22 are available, including the "R" (no sights, only the scope rings), "S" (with only the sights and no scope rings), and an "RS" version (with both iron sights and scope rings).

The 77/22 is simply "loved" by most of those who own it. It makes an excellent .22 bolt-action sniper rifle, carrying a very low price tag and a lot of quality when compared to many similar rifles.

Vaime Mark 3

While little information is available about the Vaime Mark 3 at the time of this writing, the rifle is known to be made for actual use as a sniper weapon. The bolt-action Mark 3 is currently being imported into the United States by North American Sales, International. The rifle has an integral silencer, semi-pistol grip stock, and an integral folding stock.

Specifications for .22 LR Rifles

Name	Barrel Length (in.)	Weight Unloaded (lbs.)	Length (in.)	Magazine Capacity	Name	Barrel Length (in.)	Weight Unloaded (lbs.)	Length (in.)	Magazine Capacity
Beretta Super Sport X	23.6	7.2	42.3	5, 10	Marlin 780	22	5.5	41	7
Beretta Olimpia X	23.6	8.1	42.9	5, 10	Marlin 781	22	6	41	17
F.I.E. GR-8	19.5	4	38.5	14	Marlin 782	22	6	41	7
F.I.E. Model 122	21	5.5	39	6, 10	Marlin 783	22	6	41	12
Field Arms Mark 3	20	7	40	6	Mitchell AK-22 (.22 LR)	16.5	3.1	38	29
Jäger AP-74	20	6.5	38.5	18	Mitchell AK-22 (.22 WMR)	16.5	3.1	38	10
Kimber Model 82B	22	6.25	40.5	5	Mitchell Galil (.22 LR)	16.5	5.7	36	29
Marlin 25/25M	22	5.5	41	7	Mitchell Galil (.22 WMR)	16.5	5.7	36	10
Marlin 25MB	16.25	4.75	35.25	7	Ruger 10/22	18.5	5	37.25	10
Marlin 60/990	22	5.5	40.5	18	Ruger 77/22	20	5.75	39.75	10
Marlin 70	18	5	36.5	7					
Marlin 70P	16.25	3.75	35.25	7					
Marlin 75C	18	5	36.5	14					

Note: The weight of the above rifles does not include the scope since these rifles are normally sold without scopes.

8

Scopes

Next to the rifle and its ammunition, a good scope is the most essential tool for the sniper. While modern rifle scopes have become extremely accurate and have optics that snipers of World War I and World War II would have killed for, they still aren't as tough as one might hope and are one of the potentially weak links of many sniper rifle systems. While rubber armor and heavier construction have improved the durability of many scopes, they are still rather fragile compared to the rifles on which they are mounted. In the near future, sniper rifles may be developed with a carrying handle/shield extending around the scope to protect it; until then, snipers have to baby these precise instruments from the bumps and jars they will receive when in use.

Mounting a scope on a sniper rifle designed after sporter actions is usually a matter of simply getting the right height scope rings; with sniper rifles based on military rifles, things are a bit more complicated. Generally, however, suitable scope mounts are available from the rifle or scope vender. For those creating their own sniper weapon based on a reworked military rifle, the B-Square Company is generally a good place to look, since it sells good mounts for nearly every type of readily available military rifle.

There are two schools of thought concerning whether a variable or fixed power scope is better for sniper use. Fixed scopes are generally tougher, and most of the money spent for one is for the optics of the piece rather than for the optics and a camming system. But, the fixed scope is . . . fixed.

Variable scopes allow the sniper to have a wider field of view with a lower setting so that targets can be engaged quickly. The higher settings can be used to inspect and carefully locate a target, ensuring that the sniper gets the right target and the shot itself is very precise. While variable scopes of the past tended to change their point of impact as the magnification changed, modern, quality scopes don't have that problem.

The sniper will have to decide what is best for his tastes (or settle with what he is issued). Whether using fixed or variable scopes, it is also important to remember that the buyer generally gets what he paid for when it comes to scopes, so care must be taken to stick with brand names. One should expect to shell out some money for good quality.

When a variable scope is purchased, it should be checked immediately to be sure its zero doesn't change with its setting. A good way of doing this is to mount the scope on the rifle, clamp the rifle in a barrel vise or similar arrangement so that it can't move, look at a distant target through the scope and zero in on it, and finally change the settings while checking to be sure the scope stays zeroed at each magnification. If the scope doesn't hold its zero while the rifle is clamped in place, it should be returned to the manufacturer for replacement (which most manufacturers do for free). After the rifle has been in use a while, it is also wise to run

For those creating sniper guns from military rifles, suitable scope mounts are generally available from B-Square. Shown is an HK-91 with the company's mount, which does not require gunsmithing. Photo courtesy of B-Square.

this test again.

"Quick-release" scope mounts which purport to let the user remove a zeroed scope and then remount it later without a loss of zero generally aren't all that dependable. They will get the sniper back on the target, but chances are good that the zero won't be perfect. Therefore, anyone planning to take a scope off their rifle should plan on having to rezero it upon remounting.

Whether variable or fixed, most scope failures are actually due to improper scope mounting. There are two "tricks" necessary for mounting a scope so it will hold its zero. The first necessitates that the sniper (or armorer) use Loctite on screws holding the scope in the rings and the mount to the rifle. The second is for him to place grit (from fine sandpaper) inside the front scope ring to keep the scope "welded" in place. (The sniper should be sure that eye relief and other settings are proper before having anything "permanently" put into place.)

Heat from the sun can cause scope mounts and

scope rings to expand enough to throw off the zero. A sniper's veil or other cloth should be placed over a scope rather than allowing it to sit in the sun. When possible, both for the scope's sake as well as to improve camouflage, the sniper should try to remain in shaded areas.

When a scope is mounted, care must be taken to keep its reticles properly aligned vertically and horizontally. Failure to do so will cause a slight diagonal shift as any changes are made in the scope to compensate for windage or bullet drop.

It is best to avoid "see-through" scope rings which allow a shooter to use iron sights with the scope in place, since a proper cheek weld is impossible with such an arrangement. See-through rings are of use, however, with very large diameter scopes which don't clear the rifle's barrel or receiver with standard rings. When high rings are used, a high cheek pad on the rifle's stock will make a good cheek weld possible. While this arrangement causes the sniper's head to be a bit more exposed when shooting, the advantage lies in the more controlled

The Colt AR-15 lends itself to easy scope mounting. The mount shown here, sold by B-Square, is attached through the small hole found on AR-15 carrying handles. The rifle shown here is an AR-15 A1 Sporter. Photo courtesy of B-Square.

recoil and quicker follow-up shots, since the rifle barrel doesn't leap skyward so much with each shot.

Most modern sniper scopes incorporate some type of bullet-drop compensator into their design. These devices raise or lower the scope's zero according to the bullet's ballistic arch at the range of the target. For these to work, it is necessary for the shooter to find the correct range. This is generally done by bracketing the target with part of the reticle or other stadia marks. Because a man looks smaller as his distance from the shooter becomes greater, scales can be created to give the sniper the distance to his target according to the power which has been used to bracket him in the reticle.

Some bullet-drop compensating "variable" scopes, like the Leatherwood ART series, have the bullet drop cammed and automatically coupled to the ranging/magnification wheel, so that all that needs to be done is to bracket the target. This makes the scope quick to use, but the user either has no control over the magnification when the shot is fired (as with early models of the ART scope) or he must uncouple the scope ring before changing magnification if he wishes to maintain his zero.

Variable scopes which give a shooter a choice of magnification demand that the shooter first bracket the target, adjust a separate knob for the bullet drop, and then adjust the scope's magnification to suit his taste. The scope's extra flexibility costs the sniper in the time it takes to get it ranged in on target.

Scopes also sometimes generate bullet-drop compensation or give the shooter a way to figure range through a series of markings or circles built onto the vertical cross hair which allow the shooter to bracket his target. The Shepherd line of scopes is perhaps the best example of this method of figuring distance and bullet drop; these scopes allow the shooter to bracket his target with the zero point being at the same circle used in bracketing.

There are huge numbers of scopes available in the sporting market which are readily adaptable for use with sniper rifles. When choosing a sporter scope, it is wise to pay attention to the magnification *and* the width of view. The magnification is given first and the field of view second. For example, a 2.5x32 scope will offer magnification which makes the target appear 2.5 times as large as it is to the naked eye, while the field of view will be about 32 feet wide; a 2.5x40 will offer the same magnification but a greater field of view, thereby making it easier to locate a target.

A variable scope will have two numbers followed by the field of view; 4-9x40, 4x9x40, or 4x-9x40 would all be a 4- to 9-power scope with 40 being the field of view width (the three different styles of denoting the variable magnifications varies from company to company).

As magnification changes, the field of view becomes narrower. For example, if a 3-9x40 scope is used, the field of view will be around 44 feet at 100 yards at the 3x power setting. At the 9x power setting, the field of view drops to just 10 feet at 100 yards. Because of its narrower field of view at higher magnifications, narrow fields of view are especially inferior for sniping at high settings. All things being equal, the wider the field of view, the better.

Many snipers will find that the very narrow field of view offered by many small "combat" scopes— many carrying well-known names—make finding a target difficult and leading a fast-moving target impossible. Although these scopes are rugged and less apt to attract attention (from another sniper), they are much less ideal for sniper use than larger sporter-style scopes. Unless such a scope is all that is available or has been "issued" to the sniper, he is wise to go with a larger scope if at all possible.

The upper limits of magnification are generally in the 9x to 12x power for most sniper use (except, perhaps, with the large-caliber .50 BMG rifles). Higher powers function best in areas with cool, dry weather. Another factor deciding the magnification of a scope is the weather; in hot or humid areas, water moisture in the air can cause high power settings to have less-than-sharp images. Heat can also create disconcerting waves and mirage.

For snipers who may use high power settings, practicing looking at a target while the scope is raised over the shooting eye will quickly teach the shooter to acquire a target even in the narrow field of view offered by more powerful scope settings.

The scope's ability to gather light can also be important, especially when shooting at dawn or dusk. In order to increase the scope's ability to pass light through its lens (and make for a brighter image in dim light), scope lenses are coated with special chemicals. One quick (and rough) way to judge these coatings is to look at your reflection in the front lens of the scope; with a good scope, the viewer's image won't reflect back, so it will seem like he's looking at a black hole. This occurs because none of the light reflects back from the lens; if the viewer can see himself clearly, the scope won't be of much use in dim light. In general, the more expensive scopes have better coatings, while the less expensive scopes skimp in this area. (Care must be taken not to get oil or cleaning fluids on a scope lens since the coatings of the lens will often be attacked by these solvents.)

Currently, the Soviet military is fielding small laser weapons which are capable of damaging the eyes. This is especially true if the sniper is looking through his scope when a laser beam (of visible or invisible infrared light) strikes it. In such a case, the sniper will suffer temporary loss of sight or even permanent blindness. Because of this threat, future military sniper scopes will probably also incorporate a laser filter into their design to protect the sniper's eye.

Finally, there is a huge array of reticles available. The best, however, seem to be the cross hairs which are fine at the very center and heavier as they radiate to the sides of the scope. The thick outer posts are easy to see in dim light; the thin, inner cross hairs do not cover up the target, so that you have a bit more precision when shooting. Posts and dots are also available and have their followers. For many snipers, though, the duplex cross-hair reticle is still the best bet; the horizontal wire with a dot or post and the pointed post versions are good runners-up.

The duplex cross hairs have very heavy posts at all four cross hairs, with very fine cross hairs being in the exact center of the scope. Range-finding scopes may place a second horizontal cross hair over the main duplex cross hair. The heavy posts of the duplex's cross hairs help at night when scopes having only thin cross hairs become impossible to use. The space between the heavy posts also can be used for range estimation.

There are a number of sporter scopes available which are suitable for sniper use. Redfield, Leupold, Beeman, Tasco, Simmons, Bushnell, and Shepherd all have fine scopes which are tough and backed by excellent service and warranties. However, there are four scope families that stand above all others for use with a sniper rifle.

With a wide field of view, the Armson Trijicon scope possesses good light-gathering abilities. Its reticles glow red in darkness due to the tritium found inside the scope. The Trijicon is shown with an Armson HK scope mounted on an HK-91 with a DTA Mil/Brake.

One of these is the new series of Trijicon scopes offered by Armson. These scopes have very large fields of view as well as good light-gathering abilities. However, the real advantage is seen when it gets so dark that the reticles of most scopes become invisible. The reticles of the Trijicon glow red, due to a small amount of tritium placed inside them. A new version of the Trijicon, the "Spectrum," gives the sniper a choice of red, green, or amber reticle color at night. It also allows for the cross hairs to be daylight-illuminated when firing at a dark target, where the normally black cross hairs may be hard to see. Optional rubber eye pieces are available for all models to help minimize the effects of light in the sniper's area. These features make the Trijicon scopes very useful in all but very dark environments.

The Trijicon scopes are available in the following configurations: 4x40 and 6x56 in fixed powers and 1.5-5x32, 2-7x40, and 3-9x56 in the variable scopes. (The large diameter of the 6x56 and 3-9x56 require "high" rings for mounting on many sporter-style rifles.) Prices range from about $200 to $465, depending on the model.

Another excellent line of scopes for some types of sniper use is the Bushnell Banner Lite-Site scope line. These are standard scopes except that they have a small electrical diode in them. When turned on with a switch at the top of the scope, this diode forms a point of red 2-1/2 MOA dot at the center of the cross hairs. The Banner variable 3-9x power scope is a scope to consider if money is limited and low-light use is anticipated.

Shepherd Scopes also offers several models suitable for sniper use which have a series of range-finding circles. These circles allow the shooter to

Tasco has a large number of variable scopes (like this IR 3-9x40 WA shown on the Colt AR-15 A2 H-BAR) which are ideal for sniper work and carry a low price tag. Note the Aimpoint scope mount, Cherokee cheek pad, and DTA Mil/Brake.

estimate the range at which he will be shooting and then compensate for bullet drop. (The Shepherd sighting ring range estimation system appears to be based on a system which was first pioneered by the Ranger II developed by Jim Leatherwood.) Among the Shepherd scopes which would be suitable for sniper use are the 3940-E Arounder (3-9x40) and 310-MOA (3-10x40).

Finally, a company to check when looking for a sniper-style scope is Tasco. This company has a large number of variable scopes as well as scopes with such features as illuminated reticles, 30/30 range-finding reticles (which are adaptable to use with human targets), and bullet-drop compensator scopes. One place to start looking is at the Tasco IR 3-9x40 WA scope, though many snipers may find other Tasco models more appealing.

There are a number of military scopes designed for sniping use in addition to the sporter scopes mentioned above. Unfortunately, some, like the Steiner 4x24 NATO, have terribly narrow fields of view. Others, like the Colt 3x and 4x power scopes and the Beeman SS-2 (the SS-2L with available-light illuminated reticle) have passably wide fields of view and will do in a pinch. Small scopes, by and large, have small fields of view, which are, of course, restrictive for sniper use. Fortunately, there are several excellent large military sniper scopes.

Among the first scopes designed specifically for sniper use (rather than being an off-the-shelf sporter scope) was the Leatherwood ART (Automatic Ranging Telescope) developed by James Leatherwood. This scope was used on the U.S. M-21 sniper rifle. It was usually built around a modified Redfield variable scope (with Weaver and Realist scopes sometimes being used), but had a Leatherwood-designed bullet-drop compensator cam, which raised or lowered the rear of the scope, coupled to the variable magnification knob. This made it possible to bracket a man (from his belt to the top of his head with some models and by his width with other ARTs) in the reticle space between the heavy bars of the cross hairs by varying the magnification and having the bullet drop automatically compensated for when the rear of the scope was raised or lowered. While this made it impossible for the sniper to choose his magnification when firing on a target, the fact that larger magnification was needed for more distant targets made the setup a good compromise. (In later ARTs designed by Leatherwood, the bullet drop cam could be disconnected so that the scope could be used first to compensate for bullet drop and then, if time permitted, the cam ring could be uncoupled and the scope used as a conventional variable.)

A series of scope variations has been created by Leatherwood and, for a time in the early 1980s, he marketed them through a company formed with his brother, Charles Leatherwood, and Roy Riddle. Ranges and cams of these scopes vary according to the type of ammunition used with the rifle and the scope model. In addition to an ART I and ART II, Leatherwood contracted Weaver to produce a less expensive MPC (Military/Police/Civilian) model. This scope came with a table which showed the buyer how to recalibrate the scope for use with one hundred different types of chamberings/loads. Unfortunately for the Leatherwood Company, demand for the scopes was never great. Once U.S. Army orders were filled and the Marines adopted the Unertl scope, the Leatherwood Company was forced to discontinue business.

Springfield Armory produces a number of match or sniper rifles. The company is currently offering an ART scope of its own, the ART IV, for use with its rifles as well as most others. The ART IV operates identically to the Leatherwood ART scopes except that the Springfield scope has a second set of cross hairs which stay centered on the one-hundred- to two-hundred-yard zero mark. The ART IV also carries a price tag that is several hundred dollars below that of the original Leatherwood ART scopes, making it more or less of a bargain for those needing an ART scope. (Springfield also offers a version that can be used with the .270, .308 Winchester, .30-06, .300 Winchester Magnum, and other rifles, but not with the .223.)

The Israeli Military's Nimrod scope is totally different from the ART scopes. The Nimrod is a fixed power 6x40 scope with a duplex-like arrangement of cross hairs (except for the top vertical cross hair, which is unthickened at its top). In the area below the thin, center cross hair there are small calibration/grid markings which allow the sniper to estimate range by bracketing his target (with markings to allow bracketing from two hundred to one thousand meters in two-hundred-meter increments). This done, the sniper then manually changes the elevation drum according to his ranging (a calibration mark below the cross hair is used at nine hundred and one thousand meters).

One interesting deviation from the norm with the Nimrod scope is the placement of the windage knob on the left of the scope so that ejected

Though its operation is identical to that of the Leatherwood ART scope, Springfield Armory's ART IV scope has a second set of cross hairs which remain centered on the one-hundred- to two-hundred-yard zero. Photo courtesy of Springfield Armory.

cartridges from semiauto rifles won't collide with it. At the time of this writing, Magnum Research is importing the Nimrod for sale in the U.S. While the Nimrod scope is quite accurate, it is a bit slower than some others when it comes to compensating for bullet drop.

The Unertl scope (made by John Unertl Optics Company of Pittsburgh) has been adopted by the U.S. Marines for use on their M40-A1 sniper rifle. The scope has a solid steel tube (rather than the standard aluminum used with most scopes) which gives it a rather hefty weight of 2.2 lbs. The lenses are coated with a new material which allows 92 percent of the light hitting the scope to continue on through, making the Unertl among the brightest scopes available. The Unertl's ballistic cam, mounted in its elevation turret, is calibrated exactly to the Marines match ammo, so that it gives very exact zeros out to yards. To give the sniper additional accuracy, a secondary turret is used to fine-tune the ballistic cam to compensate for variations in individual lots of ammunition. Both elevation and windage readings are given *inside* the scope's field of view so that a sniper need not remove his eye from the scope to see what the Unertl's settings are; if the rifle is used in dim light and the scale is impossible to see, the elevation and windage knobs make easily-felt clicks so that a sniper can keep track of how much change is being made.

Zeroing the Unertl is accomplished by using an "L" wrench and a screwdriver, so that it is nearly impossible to "dezero" the scope in the field by accident. The scope uses duplex cross hairs, with four small dots on the horizontal hair to allow for estimating leads when moving targets are engaged. ART-style bracketing is used to compensate for bullet drop out to one thousand yards.

Leupold & Stevens, Inc., also makes a line of scopes designed specifically for sniper use marketed under the "Ultra" trademark. These scopes come with all-steel bases and steel rings which index on the surface of the mounting base to provide good retention of zero when the scope is removed and then remounted. The adjustment knobs on the Ultra scopes are oversized so that they can be easily manipulated, and the multi-coatings on the lenses give them very good light-gathering abilities.

Ultra scopes come in several models. The M1 is available in 10x, 16x, and 20x magnification with greater elevation than is found with other scopes so that bullet drop can be readily adjusted for even the most extreme ranges. Clicks made in adjusting

the scope are readily discernible by touch as well as being audible in quiet environments. The M2 is a 10x power scope which is designed for airborne or other abusive use and has special range-finding stadia lines which allow bracketing a target to judge its range. The M3 series has 10x power and has a ranging dial (available with a .308 or .300 Winchester Magnum calibration).

New technology is constantly being adapted to military use, and several devices are convenient for some sniper situations. Perhaps the most spectacular of these is the laser. This device creates a tight beam of coherent light (generally red) which is very intense and which spreads out very slowly. While a beam from a flashlight may spread out to a radius of several feet over a distance of several yards, the laser beam will still be about the same size for thirty yards or so and spread out to a diameter of only a few feet at two hundred yards. By mounting a laser on a rifle, it is possible to have its beam pinpoint the spot—within several inches—of where the rifle's bullet will be impacting over the first one hundred yards. In effect, the laser gives a sniper a "quiet, nonlethal" first shot to see where his real shot will be impacting. It also allows the shooter to fire from the hip or other position without using sights or a scope.

Care must be taken with lasers, since the light from them is so intense that it might damage one's retina. A sniper should treat the area where the beam comes out of a laser the way he does the muzzle of a loaded rifle. Also, the sniper should bear in mind that water, mirrors, and chrome can reflect the laser beam back into his eyes or those of someone else.

Lasers also have several drawbacks: they can generally be seen by the target as well as anyone ahead of the sniper. Therefore, the laser must be switched on only for a few moments to engage an enemy and then switched off immediately. Lasers also create visible beams of light in fog or smoke and are readily seen by night-vision equipment. Perhaps the greatest drawback is the fact that lasers virtually vanish in bright sunlight. This limits their use to indoors or during twilight or night (times, it should be noted, when most optical rifle scopes are nearly useless). Because of these considerations, a laser is more suited to police-sniper use than to the military sniper and to situations where very quick and momentary target acquisition is needed.

The fact that the "target" can see the laser dot is not without its advantages for police use. The red laser dot, when seen on a person by those around him, has a very sobering effect. Police snipers have had more than one suspect quickly surrender when he's realized just how close to death he is once he spots the red dot on his chest. Therefore, while lasers do not have the autonomy of a standard scope, they do have a greater deterrent effect.

Infrared lasers which produce a beam invisible to the naked eye are available to military users. A sniper using one of these wears special goggles to see the laser's spot. The greatest drawback of these lasers, however, is the price tag for the entire system: costs often run as high as $15,000.

There are a number of companies producing lasers. Currently, one of the smaller and least expensive lasers—and also one of the toughest— is manufactured in England and distributed in the U.S. by Avin Industries as the Lasersight LS 45. This little unit is easily mounted on Weaver-type scope bases, and the company has an attachment which will enable the unit to be placed on the optical scope mounted on a rifle. Such a scope mount would be ideal since it would allow the rifle to be used when the laser was not suitable, while also having the laser in place and zeroed should it be needed. Zeroing the scope-mounted laser would be simple: the sniper would sight through the scope at a target and turn on the laser, which would then show how far it needed to be moved to be brought into zero.

The LS-45 has elevation and windage screws exactly like those on most scopes and has a small switch on the end of a cord. The switch can be attached to the sniper rifle's grip so that it can be easily activated with the thumb or fingers. The LS-45 weighs less than twelve ounces; this weight includes its two standard 9-volt alkaline transistor radio batteries (readily available almost anywhere). The LS-45 uses a divergent laser beam which is a small dot at close ranges and three inches wide at one hundred yards; it has a useful range of five hundred yards at night. The unit works well in any area which isn't in the sun (i.e., at night or indoors).

While the previous generation of lasers designed for aiming rifles was much larger and bulkier, needed special batteries, and cost between $2,000 and $3,000 each, the LS-45 costs under $500, making it affordable to many needing a laser sight.

Another optical device that is useful for the sniper in very dim light is the night-vision scope. There are two types of night-vision scopes: passive and active.

Active night-vision devices date back to World War II, when both the United States—using the infrared M3 Sniperscope—and the Germans—with their Vampir sight—developed equipment that enabled them to see in the dark. Active devices are generally heavier and have a shorter range. The big mark against them is that they must have an infrared light source to illuminate the area being viewed. This light source is readily seen with other active or passive systems, making the user of an active scope a ready target for another sniper. Because of this, the active system is not used by any military power other than the Soviet Bloc countries—and it's being phased out there. An active system might be a consideration with police snipers, however, especially since active scopes are a bit less expensive.

The passive scopes were perfected during the Vietnam era and proved to be quite valuable to U.S. snipers. Passive devices use available light, by which it is too dim for the human eye to see. City glow, moonlight, or even starlight is made visible on the TV-like screen of a passive scope. The passive scope's big plus is that its range isn't as limited as that of an active night-vision device and, most important, the passive system can't be easily detected when in use.

Unlike an active system, which can work in complete darkness, a passive system must have some light in order to work. On rare occasions—such as an extremely cloudy night when the moon isn't out or in a closed, dark room—the scopes won't allow the user to see anything.

There are two generations of passive night-vision devices. The first generation works well provided it isn't used to view areas which are partially lit; doing so creates momentary streaking and blooming for anywhere from a fraction of a second to a full second making it easy to lose a target. The reason the first generation is still used is that it is less expensive to purchase and often the need to view areas with lights is not required.

Second-generation equipment can be used at night in areas where there are a few streetlights or battlefield flares. They can also be used during the daytime with a special filter (though this isn't ideal). Passive units can be quickly put out of action by exposing the lens to a bright light while the unit is on. Always mount the protective covers during the daytime, even if the unit is turned off.

While lighter than active equipment, passive scopes are still heavy and are best used when a sniper is working close to his home base. Good passive rifle scopes cost between $2,000 and $15,000, with active scopes ranging anywhere from $500 to $1,000. Both generally need special scope mounts, though NATO is currently standardizing its military night-vision equipment so that it can be used with its standard mounting bases. Among the better passive scopes are the Litton M-845, SECO NVS-520, and VARO AN/PVS-4.

Though not currently available for rifle use, thermal-imaging units are starting to show up on military vehicles, so it's probable that technological advances will bring about even smaller versions of this device which will be suitable for use on a sniper rifle

The advantages of thermal-imaging scopes would be that they could "see" thermal or infrared sources (which are created by radiated heat). The thermal imager could, in theory, also see through thin coverings of vegetation or other material and could see through many types of camouflage. It might even be capable of seeing hot spots where troops o. equipment have been sitting, thereby giving the user a clue as to the presence of an enemy.

Regardless of the scope used, the sniper must take care to zero it in accurately. While the 25-yard zero may work well with military rifles, zeroing a scoped sniper rifle in at twenty-five yards is only useful for getting the rifle onto the target for precise zeroing. Errors of just a fraction of an inch at twenty-five yards can mean major errors at two hundred yards and missed targets at extreme ranges. The sniper should zero in at one hundred yards (or one hundred meters, depending on the range). He should adjust his scope for two hundred yards and check it for accuracy there and on out to other

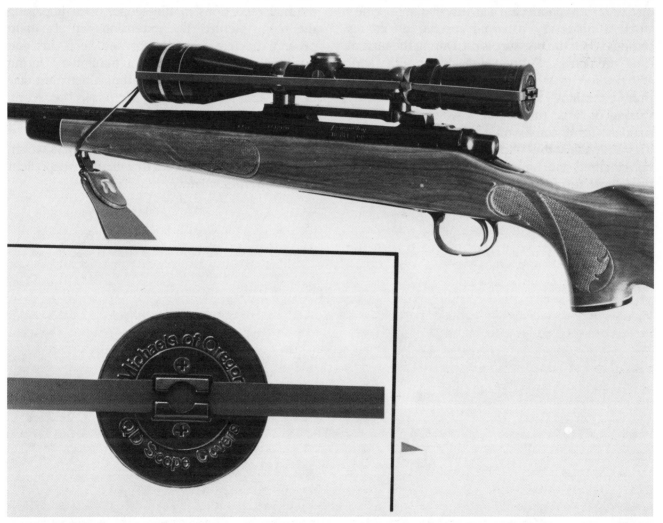

Uncle Mike's scope covers protect expensive sniper scopes from the elements. The covers, which come in a number of sizes, are designed to stay with the scope (note the bands just behind the rear scope ring and the sling swivel). The rifle shown here is the Remington 700. Photo courtesy of Michaels of Oregon.

ranges, time permitting.

Preliminary sighting in with bolt-action rifles and such weapons as the AR-15, FN LAR, and Heckler & Koch rifles can be done by removing the rifle's bolt and sighting a distant target through the rear of the receiver, comparing that to where the scope's cross hairs are. Once this zeroing is done, the rifle will generally be at least on the target when it's being zeroed by firing shots.

When zeroing the scope (as well as using it in the field), the sniper should take great care to keep his cheek weld consistent and to have the shooting eye centered behind the scope.

The sniper should also take care to mark on the scope where the actual zero is on both the windage and elevation dials so that he doesn't lose track of them in the field. Dial settings for bullet drop compensation and windage should all be placed on a waterproof note card and attached to the rifle's stock if necessary to avoid making erroneous settings when the pressure is on. During the mental (and often physical) strain of making an actual shot at a live foe, it is easy to make a mistake or have trouble recalling exact settings.

Long or large turret covers which replace the standard turret knobs on a scope make it easier to quickly adjust the "click" settings. They also stick up, catching and bumping on things a bit more than short turrets. Therefore, extra care must be taken with them. Care should also be taken to check that lock screws on turrets remain tight after the rifle has traveled a lot or has been shot several times.

Scope lens should be kept clean. A clean camel's hair brush or a photographic "squeeze-bulb" brush are both ideal for removing dust from a lens without scratching it. Cloth or paper should not be used to clean a lens. Even the soft lens cloth included with many scopes should be used only if the shooter is certain it is absolutely free of grit. One tiny bit of sand moved about on the lens during cleaning will quickly ruin a scope.

Although most scopes come with a built-in sun shade, an extended sun shade is often useful on a sniper scope. One can keep the sun from glaring on the front of the scope, thereby making a mirror-like signal to alert an enemy of the sniper's presence. The shade can also prevent glare, which causes internal reflections in the scope, often impairing the scope picture. The extension will also help protect the lens from bumps and keep dirt and fingerprints on the lens to a minimum. During extended shooting (or when the sniper must stay in the sun for extended periods), the scope extension also helps reduce heat shimmer.

A few scopes come with scope extensions or have them available as options. Generally, however, the sniper will be forced to create an expedient extension from whatever is at hand.

9

Accessories

As is the case with other rifles, there is a wealth of accessories for the sniper rifle. Care must be taken by the sniper not to overburden himself with unneeded equipment; doing so will limit the speed at which he can travel and react to danger, as well as making it harder for him to conceal himself.

With this in mind, there is no "set" of equipment which a sniper should have. It will vary from sniper to sniper, and even from one sniping mission to another.

There are also a number of accessories and other gear which will aid in practice and help keep the sniper rifle functional. These are also important and should not be overlooked by those setting up a sniper program or trying to develop their shooting skills.

Air Rifles

Because there are few places in populated areas where one can shoot even a .22 rifle, many snipers have discovered that an air rifle is a very useful way to perfect shooting techniques, hone good habits, and keep in practice. Modern, accurate air rifles are available with good trigger pulls and, when equipped with a good scopes, demand that shooters use proper technique in order to hit their marks. The low cost per shot encourages a lot of practice without the worry of expense, since even quality pellets are dirt cheap.

There are various types of air rifles, including CO_2 (carbon dioxide), spring-powered, and pneumatic. While all are good, the pneumatic is often best for sniper practice, because its power can be varied by the number of pumps used, making it possible to use the rifle indoors on small, homemade ranges (using small targets and short ranges) or outdoors at longer ranges with more pumping. Pneumatic actions don't have the violent spring or bounce that spring-powered guns have, so that expensive shock-proof scopes don't have to be purchased for the practice air gun. If a rifle scope is also used on the air gun, it won't be damaged. Lighter trigger pulls are also easier to achieve on pneumatic rifles, which helps keep the manufacturing costs down while still giving the sniper a pull which won't be distracting.

Air guns in the U.S. are readily available in both .177 and .22 calibers. Most shooters will probably prefer the .177 since it has a flatter trajectory.

Currently, Daisy Manufacturing air guns are the best buys on the market for snipers looking for practice pellet guns. The Daisy company has a full line of rifles, including guns for the beginner, adult "plinking" rifles, and expensive target guns.

Good choices for sniper practice are the Powerline 860, the Powerline 880, the 970, the 953, and top-of-the-line Gamo 126 (which is imported from Europe by Daisy). All are pneumatic .177 rifles (with .22 counterparts available for the first three). Prices vary from less than $50 up to over $250 for the above-noted rifles, so that there is practically a model for every budget.

The 860 and 880 have plastic stocks, while the 970 is a wooden-stocked version of the 880. All three rifles can be used with lead .177 pellets; the 860 and 880 can even be used with BBs by those who really want to fire with minimal expense with only a slight loss in accuracy. The 970 has a heftier feel to it, thanks to a heavier wooden stock. It would be the first choice from this group for most sniper practice.

The 953 is a quality target rifle with a rail for scope use and very good iron sights (with a choice of four interchangeable inserts). Based on the action of the 970, the 953 needs only one pump to charge its air reservoir, giving a very constant speed to pellets. Also helping it achieve good accuracy is a Lothar Walther barrel and a 4.5-pound trigger pull. (The U.S. Army is now purchasing a special version of this rifle, the 853, for use in training shooters.)

The Gamo 126 has seen use in Olympic shooting matches because of its accuracy. Like the 953, it takes only one pump to fill its air reservoir (but it still has the low recoil and minimal vibration of a pneumatic). The Gamo 126 owner has a choice of three sight apertures, and the trigger and butt plate are both adjustable for a real custom feel. The one-piece hardwood semipistol grip stock has stippling for a good hold, and the Gamo's total weight is 10.6 pounds, giving it the feel of a real sniper rifle.

Air-rifle practice can be carried out on anything from paper targets to empty .22 LR cartridges. Some shooters even go on "hunts" and stalk grasshoppers or other insects in their backyards. The main thing is that the sniper learns how to judge the precise moment when the scope hairs line up on target, when is the time to pull the trigger, and how to call his shots so that he learns to "feel" when a shot is right.

All in all, the air rifle provides the shooter with a lot of good practice where none is otherwise done—at bargain-basement prices and with minimal noise and bother.

Binoculars

One of the most important accessories which a sniper can have is a good pair of binoculars. This vital piece of equipment will enable him to scan an area for targets nearly as quickly as with the naked eye, while giving more magnification and detail than is otherwise possible. Although a rifle scope can be used to pick out possible targets, use of binoculars is generally quicker and much less fatiguing to the eyes.

The choice of binoculars is generally best left to the sniper (and/or his spotter); binoculars should, however, have a wide field of view, should be of a low magnification (so that the "wobble" from being hand-held won't obscure details), and have coated lenses capable of gathering light during dusk viewing. Carrying cases, lens caps, rubber "armor," and ranging systems are also very useful on binoculars used by a sniper. "Mini" binoculars are best left to sporting events; they generally have too narrow a field of view to be of use for spotting potential targets and have poor light-gathering abilities.

Among the best binoculars which might be considered for sniper use are the Steiner Commander and Military-Marine (both 7x50), and the Tasco Explorer (which is nearly identical to the Steiner binoculars except for a price tag several hundred dollars lower). The Steiner binoculars have been selected as the U.S. Army's M22 binoculars; the military version is nearly identical to the commercial binoculars except for a laser filter which has been added (Soviet laser weapons designed to damage the eyes of those viewing a target through optical systems will undoubtedly dictate the addition of laser filters to rifle scopes as well in the near future).

The Tasco Explorer has a number of useful features, including an internal bearing compass, range finder, rubber armor, rubber eye cushions, and lens caps which are attached to the binoculars to prevent their loss. Both the Steiner and Tasco scopes are available at most sporting goods stores as well as from Brigade Quartermasters.

Bipods

Unfortunately, many bipods are suitable only for displaying a rifle and are nearly worthless when precise shooting is needed. Quality bipods, though, can be useful to many snipers who have the time to carefully set up a position and want to have their rifle as steady as possible when the time comes to fire.

Care must be taken not to add a bipod to the barrel of a rifle which may suffer from barrel flex. AR-15s, FN LARs, and Heckler & Koch rifles all have potential problems with this even in their HBAR versions. If a barrel flexes, a bipod can change the point of impact by causing the barrel to move upward slightly when in the prone position. Should a shot be fired from a standing position with a bipod

The spring-loaded telescoping legs on this aluminum bipod by Harris Engineering can either lock in an open or folded position. Photo courtesy of Harris Engineering.

fitted in place, the barrel will flex downward ever so slightly. These changes in the direction in which the barrel is pointed may translate into several inches up or down when shots are fired.

One way to avoid this problem with these firearms is to mount the bipod toward the receiver. Unfortunately, such bipods aren't readily available and will need to be improvised. (With the AR-15, it is also possible to get fixed fore grips that allow the barrel to float freely inside them; mounting the bipod to the fore grip will prevent it from flexing the barrel and will allow the use of a tight sling hold if the sling is mounted to the fore grip.)

The metal clothespin bipod used by the U.S. military is a very poor bipod. Made of stamped metal, it rusts easily and is hard to carry when not in use. A better variation on the clothespin design is available in Ram-Line's tough plastic Universal bipod, which costs only about $10 and can be quickly mounted or taken off the rifle. Made of a 66 percent nylon/33 percent glass-fiber mixture, the bipod is quite strong; it also has locking lugs on its feet, making it possible to lock the legs together and carry the bipod in a pocket.

One very good bipod to be found on a lot of sniper rifles is manufactured by Harris Engineering, and costs about $44.50. The aluminum bipod has spring-loaded, telescoping legs which lock in either an open or folded position, depending on the sniper's needs.

The Harris bipod mounts into detachable sling mount holes or, if the metal ring of the sling swivel is removed and the hole enlarged slightly, into most military rifle sling swivel posts. Once mounted in the sling swivel hole, the bipod can be tightened into place with a set screw so that it is wobble-free. (A ring on the bipod allows the sniper to use a sling to carry the rifle if needed.)

The Harris bipod is offered in two styles, one with standard-length legs and another with extra-long legs that allow shooting from a sitting position. In general, the low bipod style is better suited for most sniping use and gives much steadier support.

There are any number of field expedients which can be used if a bipod is not in use or unavailable. Snipers in the past, for instance, have created bipods from sticks. It is often necessary to shoot from a rest (such as a tree or side of a building), using the off hand to support the rifle. Rags or a hat placed under the rifle's barrel or stock can also be used to support the rifle on window frames or the backs of chairs for those engaged in urban sniping.

Finally, it should be noted that German snipers in World War II often used the extended magazines of their semiauto rifles as a monopod. Most modern assault rifles with 20- or 30-round magazines also adapt very well to such use. New plastic magazines are especially suitable for such use; several layers of tape or a rag on the bottom of a metal magazine will minimize the chance of damaging it. (The author has used magazines as rests on modern sniper rifles to shoot sub-MOA groups; the technique works very well.)

Camouflage

Proper camouflage is essential for the sniper. Camouflage can be quite complicated—enough so that space doesn't permit covering it in detail. Suffice to say, camouflage is more art than science, and the best of camouflage can be quickly defeated by poor hiding techniques. Having absolutely no camouflage is often better than a little, since the sniper without any will use natural cover to hide himself while the person with camouflage gear tends to think that it makes him invisible, so that he will "camp out" in the open and be easily spotted by an enemy.

In general, dark colors offer more concealment than light, and camouflage created by texture (cloth strips, vegetation, rags, burlap wraps, etc.) is more effective than camo paints, tape, or expedients like mud, soot, or thin cloth covers.

To quickly camouflage the sniper's face, hunters' mesh veils are available which slip over the hat and head. One big advantage of these veils is that they break up the wearer's outline somewhat and also keep bugs away from the face—two shortcomings of camo face paint. Unfortunately, vision is somewhat restricted with a veil.

One of the best camouflage suits available to the sniper is the "Ghillie" suit (which apparently was first created in the 1800s by English gamekeepers called "Ghillies"). Though the Ghillie suit offers excellent concealment, it's also quite bulky and awkward to use, so a sniper should be certain he really needs it before wearing one into the field.

A Ghillie suit can be created by gluing or sewing strips of rags to a uniform so that the sniper is completely concealed in the rags. Though it seems that such an outfit would offer little camouflage, in fact it achieves excellent concealment because it breaks up the outline of the wearer as well as completely changing the texture normally associated with a human being or his clothing. Those viewing a person wearing a Ghillie suit tend to scan past him as they do a clump of vegetation. Provided the sniper stays in an area with vegetation and remains motionless, it is possible for him to be concealed from detection by the human eye to within just a few yards.

While commercially available from time to time, Ghillie suits are generally made by the sniper for his own use. Burlap in various muted colors is the best material for a Ghillie suit. The cloth should be cut into strips about 2 inches wide and 6 to 12 inches long; the strips should not be of uniform length or width and the edges should be allowed to unravel slightly. Strips should be "shingled" so that they overlap and care should be taken to keep the pattern as random as possible. The strips should be thinner across the front of the wearer's hat so that he can see through them without problem while still having his face concealed. Spray paint can also be used to augment the camouflage effect of the Ghillie suit if the wearer so desires.

Cheek Pad

Many snipers will find that a cheek pad is essential for proper cheek weld. One good pad is the Cheekpiece, available from Cherokee Gun Accessories for about $42. Made of urethane, it attaches to a rifle's stock by a strap or Velcro connecter.

Springfield Armory also offers a leather cheek piece designed for use with the Garand/M14 rifle; it is also readily adaptable to many other rifles. The cost is approximately $25.

Cleaning Equipment

Sniper rifles, like other firearms, can have their potential accuracy ruined in short order through improper cleaning methods. Care must especially be taken not to let cleaning rods rub against the inside of the bore at the muzzle end of the barrel; wear here causes bullets leaving the barrel to become unstable, translating into poor accuracy down range.

Perhaps the best way to avoid this problem is to obtain a cleaning kit which has a small muzzle insert through which the rod is inserted so that the rod can't touch the inside of the barrel at the muzzle. Some shooters also are able to do much the same thing by keeping their fingers around the rod at the muzzle while they push the cleaning rod with their other hand. Another good method is to clean the rifle from the breech, pushing the cleaning brush and patches toward the muzzle.

When cleaning, care must be taken not to push and pull cleaning patches through the bore since doing so may just move fouling up and down the inside of the barrel rather than removing it.

If the rifle must be cleaned in the field, cleaning kits which use steel rods are the best bet; aluminum rods and pull-through strings often pick up grit which scratches the bore and shortens its life. If the rifle will be cleaned in an environment where the rods won't become contaminated with grit, the type of kit used is pretty much up to what the sniper prefers. Aluminum and pull-through cleaning gear may actually cause less wear than steel rods in that case.

While older methods of cleaning rifles called for using a solvent to lift dirt from the bore and then using oil, modern one-step cleaners/lubricants are more ideal and do a better job of cleaning and lubricating. Perhaps the best of these is Break Free CLP. When using Break Free CLP, let the rifle sit for about twenty minutes before use, so that the lubricants can set up in the rifle.

Regardless of the lubricant used, care must be taken not to get oil on ammunition since it can quickly deactivate it or can cause dangerous pressures when a cartridge fails to grip the inside of the chamber during firing.

Once cleaning is done, care must be taken to get the last bit of oil out of the bore if the rifle is to be fired very soon. A thin coat of oil in the bore causes a deviation in bullet impact, causing the first shot to be a flier.

In very cold or sandy areas, oil on a firearm can cause the rifle's action to become very sluggish or to attract grit. In such cases, the rifle may be carried "dry" without any lubricant on it, but this can cause excessive wear, especially with semiauto actions. A better bet is to use non-oil, dry graphite lubricants like E & L Manufacturing's Gun Lube, which comes in a handy spray can. Use of Teflon or other coatings on the outside of the weapon will allow the rifle to be left unoiled, while still preventing rust.

Eye Protection

While having a cartridge blowup in a sniper rifle is rare, it isn't unheard of. Likewise, in combat (especially in urban areas), a lot of dust and even splinters of concrete and rock often fly about. Just one bit of rock, a splinter of brass, or a grain of burning powder which chances to get into a sniper's eye can mean temporary (or even permanent) loss of sight. Loss during practice can end the sniper's shooting career and, in battle, can end his life. Eye protection, both in practice and battle, is a must.

New polycarbonate sunglasses offer a terrific amount of eye protection. Currently, polycarbonate lenses in sunglasses are capable of actually stopping shotgun pellets and even some pistol bullets, giving a lot of protection while weighing very little.

Among the best polycarbonate glasses are Brigade Quartermasters' Gargoyles (which the U.S. military now allows its troops to use) and Jones Optical's wide array of stylish polycarbonate sunglasses, skiing goggles, and "combat" goggles. The price tags for these glasses are not much higher than for a pair of good nonpolycarbonate sunglasses, but the protection is much, much greater for the money spent.

With sunglasses or protective goggles, the wearer must not allow light to strike the surface of the lens, since doing so can create a bright flash that is visible for some distance. This flash can give away a sniper's position. A brimmed hat of some type will prevent this from happening.

Hearing Protection

A sniper also needs to have full use of his ears; sometimes, hearing a sound clearly will decide whether a sniper can locate an enemy or become an enemy's victim. To maintain his ability to hear well, it's important that hearing protectors be used when practicing, since even a short-barreled .22 rifle, especially on an indoor range, can take its toll on one's hearing (ear protection will also help prevent a flinch). A centerfire rifle can do measurable damage with just a few rounds fired without hearing protection. A sniper who practices without hearing protection for several years will have permanent ear damage.

Earmuffs designed to give maximum ear protection are most ideal, but even the expanding, disposable plastic plugs give a lot of protection for just a few pennies. Considering the importance of having good hearing, the expense and trouble of using hearing protection during practice will pay off during sniper combat.

Load-Bearing Equipment

A sniper who needs to carry a canteen or spare magazines may wish to use a vest-style carrying system rather than a load-bearing belt/suspender arrangement. Vests are less apt to get hung up in foliage, and the equipment carried in them can often be arranged to allow comfortable prone shooting.

Snipers may wish to use a vest-style carrying system, like this ALICE Gear LBE vest from Brigade Quartermasters, rather than a load-bearing belt/suspender arrangement. Prone shooting is easier when one shifts the load to the rear of the vest rather than to the front as shown here. Photo courtesy of Brigade Quartermasters.

There are a number of these available on the market. Israeli Military Industries designers have developed several excellent vests which are currently being marketed in the U.S. under the Uzi trademark by Brigade Quartermasters and other companies.

Many times, a sniper should consider carrying equipment in pants and jacket pockets, especially if he has a uniform with a number of pockets. The addition of a belt with a canteen, a good knife, and perhaps a pistol will allow him to travel "lean and mean."

Muzzle Brakes and Flash Hiders

Muzzle brakes reduce the recoil of a rifle by

The Uzi Commando SWAT vest is ideal for sniper use, allowing the wearer to carry a lot of equipment without getting it caught on foliage. Photo courtesy of Brigade Quartermasters.

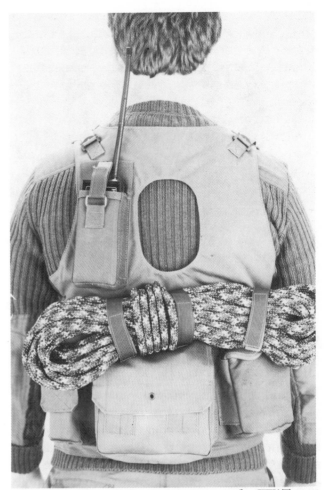

The rear view of the Uzi Commando SWAT vest by Brigade Quartermasters shows large capacity rear pockets. The vest is ideal for placement of a police radio. Photo courtesy of Brigade Quartermasters.

diverting some of the gas coming from the muzzle back toward the shooter; they work, but the price is increased muzzle blast heard by the shooter. Compensators work much the same way, but the blast is diverted upward and to the right (for right-handed shooters); this pushes the rifle in the direction opposite from that of the barrel, tending to twist the rifle during recoil. Flash hiders (also called flash suppressors) reduce the flash of the weapon in low-light conditions.

Modern flash hiders also do some compensation, and many muzzle brakes have flash hiders built into them. However, there is generally some compromise which must be made since compensation or braking tend to increase muzzle flash. While modern designs are good, no muzzle device does everything, and the sniper will have to decide what is needed and what he can do without in the way of muzzle brakes, compensators, and flash suppressors.

With the larger caliber rifles, especially the .50 BMG sniper weapons, muzzle brakes are of prime importance. These rifles generally come equipped with good muzzle brakes, though it is possible that new brakes might be created as technology becomes more refined.

Muzzle brakes can also be of great use (even on .223 rifles) since a sniper can watch his target as the bullet strikes. This enables the sniper to call his own shots during practice or to tell whether a quick follow-up shot is called for in combat.

The Soviet AK-74 was fielded with a fairly good compensator/muzzle brake, and several U.S. companies offer versions of it for the AR-15, Mini-14, and Heckler & Koch rifles. The Soviet muzzle brakes, though, are terribly noisy, can stir up dust during prone shooting, and offer very poor flash reduction (there is actually not much of a difference than when there is no flash suppressor in place).

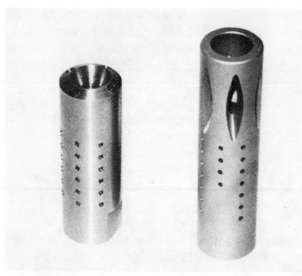

DTA Mil/Brakes from Fabian Brothers greatly reduce recoil, compensate for the barrel's upward and sideward movements, and do a good job of hiding muzzle flash. The smaller unit is designed for .223 rifles; the larger for .308s. Photo courtesy of Fabian Brothers.

Therefore, most snipers will want to steer clear of this design.

Many FN LAR versions come with a muzzle brake/flash hider (which consists of a series of holes drilled into the muzzle attachment). These work quite well and give an almost 80 percent drop in flash while also reducing recoil. Choate Machine and Tool markets a similar device for the Mini-14 and AR-15 which works equally well.

The best muzzle brake/compensator/flash hider currently available is the DTA Mil/Brake. The Mil/Brake can be adjusted for left- or right-hand use in order to compensate for barrel drift. It reduces recoil by about 47 percent on .223 rifles and almost 36 percent on .308 rifles, translating into a lot more control over the rifle when fired. While recoil reduction isn't quite as great as straight muzzle brakes (like the AK-74 style), the Mil/Brake reduces flash by about 65 percent (as opposed to 80 to 85 percent for most AR-15-style, bird-cage flash hiders). These reductions in flash make the Mil/Brake very hard to detect except in extremely dark environments. Furthermore, it doesn't kick up much dust since most of its venting of gases is upward or forward. All in all, the DTA Mil/Brake is the first choice by those needing a muzzle brake.

The DTA Mil/Brake is being marketed by the Fabian Brothers, with blued and parkerized versions for most .223 and .308 rifles going for about $30 each (while the special M14/M1A version costs

about $60). Among the rifles which DTA Mil/Brakes are made for are the AR-15/M16 (all versions), the G3/HK-91, G33/HK-93, G-41, FN LAR, AUG, Galil (.308 and .223), and M14/M21/M1A. Many sporters and other rifles can be adapted to the DTA Mil/Brake by having their barrels threaded to fit the brakes.

For those wanting maximum muzzle flash reduction and no braking or compensation, the prong-style flash hider used on early M16 rifles works with great efficiency and will almost completely end muzzle flash with a twenty-inch barrel. The catch, in addition to lack of muzzle braking, is that the prongs tend to wick in moisture on .223 rifles, so that rain or even dew from heavy vegetation can create a dangerous situation when the moisture is present in the barrel. Therefore, care must be taken when using these devices.

For those wanting maximum muzzle-flash reduction and no braking or compensation, the prong-style flash hider, like this Nil-Flash, works with great efficiency. It will nearly end muzzle flash with a twenty-inch barrel.

Currently, two different prong-style flash hiders are available commercially. One is marketed as the Vortex, and the other is known as the D.C.Brennan Nil-Flash. Both work very well. (AR-15 owners may also be able to find U.S. military-surplus prong flash hiders which have been removed from old M16 rifles and sold as scrap.)

Range Finders

While the quickest way to find the range of a shot is to use a ranging scope like the ART, range finders can also be of great use, especially by two-man sniper teams. The best range finder readily available on the commercial market is made by Ranging, Inc. Its stereoscopic system is quite inexpensive and works well with a little practice. Though not overly rugged, with a little care the

Ranging range finders will stand up well and can prove very useful to a sniper. The Ranging 1000 model gives distances out to one thousand yards (in either yards or meters—depending on the version purchased).

Sniper teams should practice with the range finder on a rifle range that has been carefully laid out or on a football field or similar area where known ranges can be used to check readings. The Ranging 1000 also has several range overlays that will allow snipers to jot bullet drop figures onto the scale so that bullet drop can be easily figured out as well.

Range finders built into binoculars are also available. While potential accuracy is not quite as great (due to reduced distance between the two viewing lenses), binoculars with range finders are often easier to use as opposed to carrying a separate range finder along with a pair of binoculars.

New laser range finders, which can be mounted on the sniper rifle, are also becoming available to military users. One example of this new devices is the Norma "Teleranger," which mounts over the sniper's scope. Once the scope is centered on target, the sniper presses a control button which causes the Teleranger to send out an invisible beam of infrared light, measuring the time it takes for the light to be reflected back to the unit. The device then shows the range in meters to the target via a small LED display at the rear of the unit. The Teleranger also tells in its display whether a second target is present, whether the target is out of range (beyond 1995 meters), and whether the batteries which power the unit are running low. The batteries themselves are readily available "AA" cells. Such small, lightweight rangers promise to give future snipers very precise ranging abilities.

Silencers

Silencers—also called sound suppressors—are occasionally found on sniper rifles. There are several reasons for this, one being that many silencers act as muzzle brakes to reduce recoil. Silencers can also help to hide muzzle blast.

Of course, centerfire sniper rifles equipped with silencers aren't very silent with regular ammunition because of the supersonic crack that a bullet makes as it cuts through the air. Silencers do, however, cut down on the muzzle noise, making it hard to locate a concealed sniper from beyond one hundred yards by the "crack and thump" method when he uses a silencer.

The sonic crack itself can also be done away with by using subsonic ammunition (which translates to heavy bullets traveling at a low speed). With a good silencer and subsonic loads, the noise of the rifle and bullet can drop to about one hundred to two hundred decibels—still noisy but quieter than the report from an unsilenced .22 rifle. For those sniping at longer ranges in relatively quiet areas, a silencer can make a lot of sense.

A number of companies offer silencers. One good source is Jonathan Arthur Ciener.

Slings

With the sniper rifle, slings are often used for more than just carrying the gun; they can also provide a rock-steady hold for shooting from the standing position. As such, however, the sling is not as essential as one might think and can even be detrimental for rifles with any sort of barrel flex problems.

Snipers who fire from the prone position or one which allows for the use of bipods, or who fire when using a tree or other object to support their rifle, find the sling can actually prove to be a nuisance. Such snipers may wish to dispense with their slings or use a sling with quick-detach swivels so that it can be quickly removed.

For rifles which suffer from barrel flex, snipers should learn to use the standing technique practiced by many target shooters who use their off hand to support the rifle from the lower side of the receiver. Standing holds which use the lower side of a military rifle's extended magazine as a support often are as quick and stationary as sling holds, as well as being a bit easier to manage with HBAR rifles.

Slings don't have to be mounted out toward the muzzle end of the rifle, either. Though mostly of an "experimental" nature, a few AR-15 and FN LAR snipers are toying with various arrangements which mount the sling around the barrel at the front of the receiver and place the supporting hand toward the barrel's receiver end. Barrel flex is minimal, while the sling can still be used to rivet the rifle in place when standing. In short, while the sling positions developed for use with World War I-vintage rifles may have merit, especially with sporter-style sniper rifles, it hardly makes sense to think that they are the best for modern semiauto military rifles.

Regardless of the sling position or style used, the nylon sling has a lot more durability and strength

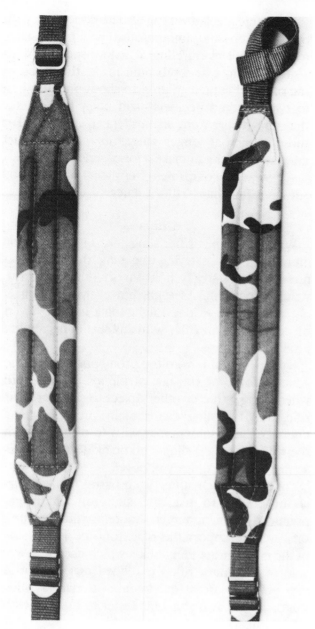

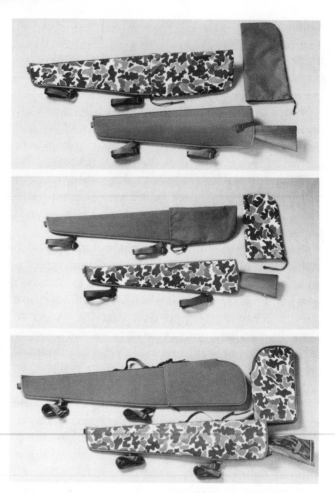

Scabbards by Uncle Mike's can double as carrying and storage cases. Removable tops found on the zippered models allow for quick access to the rifle. Uncle Mike's has three sizes to accommodate most sniper rifles. Photo courtesy of Michaels of Oregon.

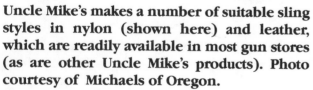

Uncle Mike's makes a number of suitable sling styles in nylon (shown here) and leather, which are readily available in most gun stores (as are other Uncle Mike's products). Photo courtesy of Michaels of Oregon.

over the long haul than its leather counterpart. Unless the sniper is going to operate in a very dry environment, he should consider using a nylon sling.

For standard-length slings, Uncle Mike's (an overall good source for slings) makes a number of suitable styles in both leather and nylon (in brown, black, and camo). These can be purchased at most gun stores.

Those wanting to stick with the traditional military sling should check out those carried by Springfield Armory, which has a Garand/M14-style leather sling for about $24 and a GI canvas sling for $10 or so.

Any metal or heavy plastic fasteners and slides should be covered with tape so that they don't hit the rifle and create noise when the sniper moves. Some thought should also be given to camouflaging the straps since they may otherwise present a dark, straight line that can be readily seen from some distance.

Scabbards and Carrying Cases

Snipers who have to travel when their rifles won't be in use will want to give some thought to a good carrying case. "Soft" cases of canvas or nylon are good for short trips when the sniper can keep track of his rifle. If the gun will be handled by baggage crews or others, a metal case is a must. The best bet is to take the sniper rifle to a large gun store and get a case that fits the rifle properly.

Soft cases which double as scabbards are available from Uncle Mike's and are ideal for snipers who may be carrying the rifle in a vehicle. The zippered scabbards have removable tops so that the rifle can be ready for quick use when it doesn't require maximum protection.

Police snipers, or snipers who take their rifles to a target range, may wish to carry their firearm in a soft case so as not to attract a lot of attention. For such occasions, Springfield Armory's Assault Rifle Cases are ideal; less-expensive alternatives are the simple nylon cases available from both Sherwood International and Parellex.

Sniper rifles should be stored in a case or other container which will "breathe," allowing air to flow around it. Tight plastic containers or "leather" vinyl cases will quickly cause a rifle to rust.

10

Sniper Development

Tactics for the sniper are rather simple: stay hidden and hit only the most important targets.

But, as good snipers know, these rules aren't all that easy to carry out. Even a small error can spell failure or even death to a sniper, since he will often be facing numerically superior forces and may even be far into enemy territory.

Good camouflage techniques (and proper use of camouflage) can help a sniper remain concealed, but it is also important for the sniper not to pick the most obvious spots from which to snipe. Landmarks, the highest point in the area, or a site having a clear view of a large area seem like logical sniper posts to those unfamiliar with wise sniper practices; spots like these quickly draw enemy anti-sniper fire, and being in such a place could quickly spell an end to a sniper's career.

Sniper posts can be very simple or extremely elaborate, depending on the time the sniper has to prepare an area and whether or not he will remain in the area. Areas with a lot of rubble or vegetation lend themselves to building more complex and permanent posts, as opposed to open stretches of land (which, in turn, often present more targets to a sniper).

Perhaps the most complex sniper camouflage posts were created on the Western Front during World War I. Sniper posts looking like fallen soldiers or horses were often created by artists working in Britain; concrete "trees" and other objects common to the battlefield were also built to allow snipers to hide where they had clear shots over the battlefield. (For a more complete look at complicated sniper posts and camouflage techniques, see *The German Sniper 1914-1945* by Peter R. Senich, available from Paladin Press.)

Whether simple or elaborate, sniping posts must give the sniper more than just a clear target. They must also allow the sniper to have a route by which to enter the post without being seen by an enemy. For military snipers, there is also a need for undetected exit should the sniper get a "hot response" from his enemies. (Police snipers often don't have to worry about being able to leave their posts undetected since a criminal or terrorist action will generally be quickly terminated. Leaving undetected by the press may, however, be a consideration.)

The post also needs to be comfortable, since the sniper may find that he needs to occupy it for long periods of time—time during which he can't move about or battle insects that seem to collect around a man trying to remain still.

If the sniper is to remain in a post for extended periods, the position needs to be larger than might otherwise be the case; normally, a sniper team consisting of two men is deployed so that one can rest while the other searches for targets. Because observation puts a lot of stress on a sniper, especially when optical equipment is used, teams of two snipers (with one observing for brief periods while the other fires the rifle) are considerably more efficient than a lone sniper trying to fill both roles. The only times that teams of men would not be employed is when manpower is very limited or when the two men might be detected.

In addition to finding targets, the observer in a two-man sniper team will help with range estimation, give corrections if a target is missed, and offer protection while his teammate is eating or sleeping. Generally, both members of the sniping team are trained as snipers.

In areas where snipers may be working in especially vulnerable positions, they are often supported by other armed personnel who can give covering fire should the snipers be detected by the enemy.

Snipers often have such secondary roles as helping to guard areas, gather intelligence, or locate targets for artillery or aircraft. Unfortunately, many military leaders use their snipers for such tasks rather than allowing the sniper to carry out his more effective task of eliminating key enemy personnel and equipment.

Because the sniper is dependent on shooting skills and the quality of his equipment, it is also essential that he has time to practice and that his weapon is regularly checked and repaired by skilled armorers. Sending a sniper out without sufficient practice or with inadequate equipment generally guarantees less-than-great success and often results in tragic failure.

While the police sniper generally has only limited time and few specified targets to deal with, the military sniper often has almost unlimited opportunities to strike targets of importance. Because of this, the sniper is often tempted to take just one more shot, and another, and another, until he is finally detected.

Such an event will usually lead to his death. To prevent this, the sniper must know when to quit. An old sage put it this way: "I only give my snipers five cartridges for their rifles when I send them out. If I do that, they'll almost always take out an important target and return. If they carry all the ammunition they comfortably can, chances are they won't come back."

Finally, the sniper must have the proper motivation and control of his psychological makeup so he understands that what he does is of prime importance and that it will save lives on his side

if he does a good job. Not just anyone is capable of striking out from a distance to cut down an opponent who is unaware of the sniper's presence. Sniper training must be done in such a manner as to remove from the program not only those who are not good marksmen but also those who may not be capable of dealing with the actual act of killing an enemy. Likewise, the sniper must be supported while he is actually carrying out his task of killing enemies and destroying enemy equipment. Thus, adequate sleep and relaxation, and the time to talk to others engaged in similar combat is of prime importance. If possible, chaplains, psychologists, and other support personnel should be available to the sniper. Using two-man sniper teams, rather than single snipers operating alone, also seems to improve the ability of the sniper to operate over long periods.

With proper tactics and support personnel, military snipers can quickly decide the outcome of a battle by cutting down the enemy's military leader or damaging vital equipment; police snipers can often cut down a criminal before he can injure innocent hostages. With one shot, a sniper can end a battle or hostage situation, preventing much suffering and saving many lives on both sides of a conflict. Because the sniper operates from a long range, the chances of his being injured (especially in police and antiterrorist operations) are low; the "bad guys" are more apt to make the supreme sacrifice when a sniper is properly deployed, since a skilled sniper is able to hit an enemy even if he is among innocent citizens.

On the field of battle, military snipers making one-shot kills are able to generate fear in enemy troops which is often out of proportion to the actual damage done; therefore, such use of snipers is both economical for the force using them and demoralizing for the enemy. By the same token, police snipers can quickly demonstrate the futility of terrorist actions and serve as a deterrent to similar future acts.

The sniper can, and often does, have a greater influence on the course of events than any other person involved in a conflict. A skilled sniper is able to reach out, almost invisibly, to cut down an enemy military leader, a terrorist surrounded by innocent hostages, or a barricaded criminal with murder on his mind.

Firearms Manufacturers and Importers

AAI Corporation
P.O. Box 6767
Baltimore, MD 21204
(Manufacturer of experimental Advanced Combat Rifle)

Armscorp of America
9162 Brookville Rd.
Silver Spring, MD 20910
(Markets Israeli M14 and FN LAR rifles as well as such surplus equipment as night-vision devices)

Barrett Firearms Mfg., Inc.
2048 Barfield Rd.
Murfreesboro, TN 37130
(Barrett 82, .50 BMG-caliber semiauto rifle)

Beretta USA
17601 Indian Head Highway
Accokeek, MD 20607
(Manufacturer of AR-70 rifle)

Browning
Route One
Morgan, UT 84050-9749
(Manufacturer of Browning A-Bolt rifle)

Colt Industries
Firearms Division
P.O. Box 1868
Hartford, CT 06101
(Manufacturer of AR-15A2, AR-15 Carbine, and military M-16)

Daisy Manufacturing Company
P.O. Box 220
Rogers, AR 72757

EMF Company, Inc.
1900 E. Warner Ave., Suite 1D
Santa Ana, CA 92705
(Importer of the AP-74, an AR-15-style .22 rifle)

Gun South
Box 6607, 7605 Eastwood Mall
Birmingham, AL 35210
(Importer of AUG rifle, FN-LAR, FNC, etc.)

Heckler & Koch
14601 Lee Rd.
Chantilly, VA 22021
(Manufacturer of HK-91, HK-93, and HK-94 rifles and accessories)

Iver Johnson
American Military Arms Corp.
2202 Redmond Rd.
Jacksonville, AR 72076
(Distributor of the Aimstar Model 5100 .50 caliber and 7.62mm "Special Application" sniper rifles)

G. McMillan & Company
21438 N. 14th Ave.
Phoenix, AZ 85027
(Maker of custom stocks and McMillan M87 .50 BMG sniper rifle)

North American Sales International
P.O. Box 90
Midland, TX 79702
(Distributor of Vaime of Finland silencers and Mark
    2 and Mark 3 rifles)

Remington Arms Company
939 Barnum Ave., P.O. Box 1939
Bridgeport, CT 06601
(Manufacturer of Model 700 and 788 rifles)

SGW
624 Old Pacific Hwy. S.E.
Olympia, WA 98503
(Manufacturer of custom AR-15s, gun parts,
    accessories, and 9mm conversion units for the
    AR-15, as well as such target barrels as the new
    fluted style for the AR-15 rifle)

Springfield Armory
111 E. Exchange St.
Geneseo, IL 61254

(Manufacturer/distributor of M1A, M-14, M1A-A1,
    SAR-48 [FN-LAR], M1 Garand, M1 "Tanker
    Garand," Beretta BM-59, BM-59 Alpine Trooper,
    and BM-59 Nigerian model. Semiauto and
    selective-fire models of most of these are
    available.)

Sturm, Ruger & Co.
Southport, CT 06490
(Manufacturer of Model 77, 10/22, and Model 1)

Thompson-Center Arms
P.O. Box 2426
Rochester, NH 03867
(T/C Contender single-shot pistols and rifles with
    interchangeable barrels)

US Repeating Arms Co.
275 Winchester Ave., P.O. Box 30-300
New Haven, CT 06511
(Manufacturer of Winchester M-70 rifle)

APPENDIX B

Manufacturers of Sniper Rifle Accessories

Accuracy Rifle Systems
P.O. Box 6529
Odessa, TX 79767-6529
(Accurization of Mini-14 rifles)

Aimpoint USA
203 Elden St., Suite 302
Herndon, VA 22070
(Aimpoint scopes)

Alpha Armament
105 E. Main St.
Lebanon, OH 45036
(AK-74-style muzzle brake)

Armson
P.O. Box 2130
Farmington Hills, MI 48018
(Armson O.E.G. Trijicon scopes)

Assault Systems
869 Horan Dr.
St. Louis, MO 63026
(Rifle cases and accessories)

Beeman Precision Arms
3440 Airway Dr.
Santa Rosa, CA 95403-2040
(SS-1 and SS-2 scopes and other accessories)

Brigade Quartermasters, Ltd.
1025 Cobb International Blvd.
Kennesaw, GA 30144
(Military surplus-style equipment and accessories)

B-Square Company
P.O. Box 11281
Fort Worth, TX 76109
(Scope mounts for most military and sporting rifles)

Bushnell Optical Co.
2828 E. Foothill Blvd.
Pasadena, CA 91107
(Banner and other model scopes)

Cherokee Gun Accessories
830 Woodside Rd.
Redwood City, CA 94061
(Cheekpieces for use with scope)

Choate Machine and Tool Company
Box 218
Bald Knob, AR 72010
(Manufacturer of wide range of stocks, flash suppressors, handguards, etc., for military-style rifles)

D & E Magazine Mfg.
P.O. Box 4876
Sylmar, CA 91342
(Magazines for military rifles)

D.C. Brennan Firearms, Inc.
P.O. Box 2732
Cincinnati, OH 45201
(Nil-Flash flash suppressors for military rifles)

Daisy Manufacturing Company
P.O. Box 220
Rogers, AR 72757
(Maker of soft air guns suitable for practice)

Defense Moulding Enterprises, Inc.
Box 4328
Carson, CA 90745
(Plastic magazines for HK-91, AR-15, Mini-14, etc.)

Douglas Barrels, Inc.
5504 Big Tyler Rd.
Charleston, WV 25313
(Manufacturer of stainless steel and chrome moly
  target/sniper barrels)

E & L Manufacturing
2102 W. Coolbrook
Phoenix, AZ 85023
(Rigid brass catchers and rubber butt plates and
  stock extensions for HK-91/93/94, AR-15, etc.)

Excalibur Enterprises
P.O. Box 266
Emmaus, PA 18049
(Night-vision equipment)

Fabian Brothers Sporting Goods, Inc.
3333 Midway Drive, Suite 104
San Diego, CA 92110
(DTA Mil/Brake muzzle compensator for assault
  rifles)

Feather Industries, Inc.
2300 Central Ave.
Boulder, CO 80301
(Accessories for military rifles)

Harris Engineering
Barlow, KY 42024
(Harris bipod)

Harry Owen
P.O. Box 5337
Hacienda Heights, CA 91745
(Cartridge adapters for different types of .22 rimfire
  ammunition in the Mini-14)

Insight Systems, Inc.
P.O. Box 3065 (Highway 78)
Pueblo, CO 81005
(Manufacturer of Insight Systems Model I sniper
  kit for AR-15 rifles)

JFS, Inc.
P.O. Box 12204
Salem, OR 97309
(Manufacturer of accessories for assault rifles)

Jonathan Arthur Ciener, Inc.
6850 Riverside Dr.
Titusville, FL 32780
(Manufacturer of silencers and automatic firearms)

Jones Optical
6367 Arapahoe Rd.
Boulder, CO 80307
(Polycarbonate glasses and combat goggles)

Laser Arms Corp.
P.O. Box 4647
Las Vegas, NV 89127
(Laser-sighting systems)

Laser Products
18285 Mt. Baldy Circle
Fountain Valley, CA 92708
(Laser-aiming system for sniper rifles)

Leupold & Stevens, Inc.
Government Contracts Division
P.O. Box 688
Beaverton, OR 97075
(Manufacturer of "Ultra" sniper scopes)

Magnum Research, Inc.
7271 Commerce Circle West
Minneapolis, MN 55432
(Importer of Israeli Nimrod sniper scope)

Michaels of Oregon (Uncle Mike's)
P.O. Box 13010
Portland, OR 97213
(Rifle slings, scope covers, detachable sling swivels)

Newman's GI Supply
RR #1, Box 782
Augusta, NJ 07822
(Combat support vests, military surplus gear)

Omark Industries
P.O. Box 856
Lewiston, ID 83501
(Manufacturer of Speer, CCI, RCBS, Outers, and Weaver shooting supplies and reloading equipment)

Parellex Corporation
A25 East Fourth St.
East Dundee, IL 60118
(Distributor of magazines, flash suppressors, slings, cases, scope mounts, etc.)

Phoenix Systems, Inc.
P.O. Box 3339
Evergreen, CO 80439
(Source for much hard-to-find military-/special-purpose gear, as well as tracer ammunition and Glaser Safety Slugs)

Ram-Line, Inc.
15611 West 6th Avenue
Golden, CO 80401
(Manufacturer of AR-15/Mini-14 combo mag and Mini-14 accessories, including plastic folding stock)

Ranging Inc.
90 Lincoln Road North
East Rochester, NY 14445
(Ranging 1000 range finder)

Sherwood International
18714 Parthenia St.
Northridge, CA 91324
(Distributor of rifle magazines, slings, cases, etc.)

Sierra Supply
P.O. Box 1390
Durango, CO 81301
(Cleaning equipment, Break-Free CLP, and military ammunition/magazine carrying pouches and other surplus equipment)

Smith Enterprises
325 South Westwood #1
Mesa, AZ 85202
(Vortex flash suppressors for military rifles)

Standard Equipment Co.
9240 N. 107th St.
Milwaukee, WI 53224
(Night-vision equipment)

Tasco Sales, Inc.
P.O. Box 520080
Miami, FL 33152
(Scopes and electric-dot scope sights)

APPENDIX C

Publications and Videotapes

The following books and magazines will be of interest to those needing additional information about new products and developments with regard to sniper-style rifles (as well as other firearms), ammunition, history of sniper warfare, sniper tactics, and other related subjects.

American Rifleman magazine
1600 Rhode Island Ave., NW
Washington, DC 20036

American Survival Guide magazine
McMullen Publishing
P.O. Box 15690
Santa Ana, CA 92705-0690

Assault Pistols, Rifles and Submachine Guns
Duncan Long
Paladin Press
P.O. Box 1307
Boulder, CO 80306

"Cal. 50"
Konrad F. Schreier, Jr.
Gun Digest, 1987
DBI Books
4092 Commercial Ave.
Northbrook, IL 60062

Combat Ammunition:
Everything You Need to Know
Duncan Long
Paladin Press
P.O. Box 1307
Boulder, CO 80306

Combat Loads for the Sniper Rifle
Ralph Avery
P.O. Box 857
West Seneca, NY 14224-0857

Counter Sniper Guide
Paladin Press
P.O. Box 1307
Boulder, CO 80306

Firepower magazine
Turbo Publishing
P.O. Box 270
Cornville, AZ 86325

The German Assault Rifle: 1935-1945
Peter R. Senich
Paladin Press
P.O. Box 1307
Boulder, CO 80306

The German Sniper: 1914-1945
Peter R. Senich
Paladin Press
P.O. Box 1307
Boulder, CO 80306

International Combat Arms magazine
Peterson Publishing Company
8490 Sunset Blvd.
Los Angeles, CA 90069

Marine Sniper
Charles Henderson Military Book Club
Dept. 834
Garden City, NY 11535

A Rifleman Went to War
H.W. McBride
Lancer Militaria
Box 886
Mt. Ida, AR 71957

S.W.A.T. magazine
148 South Main St.
Cottonwood, AZ 86326

S.W.A.T. Tactics
Jeffrie Jacobs
Paladin Press
P.O. Box 1307
Boulder, CO 80306

The S.W.A.T. Team Manual
Capt. Robert Cappel
Paladin Press
P.O. Box 1307
Boulder, CO 80306

S.W.A.T. Training and Employment
Steven Mattoon
Paladin Press
P.O. Box 1307
Boulder, CO 80306

Silencers in the 1980s:
   Great Designs, Great Designers
J. David Truby
Paladin Press
P.O. Box 1307
Boulder, CO 80306

Silencers, Snipers & Assassins
J. David Truby
Paladin Press
P.O. Box 1307
Boulder, CO 80306

Small Arms of the World
Edward Clinton Ezell
Stackpole Books
P.O. Box 1831
Harrisburg, PA 17105

Sniper, Counter Sniper
Mark V. Lonsdale
S.T.T.U. Training Division
P.O. Box 491261
Los Angeles, CA 90049

Soldier of Fortune magazine
P.O. Box 693
Boulder, CO 80306

Sniping—U.S. Marine Corps
Paladin Press
P.O. Box 1307
Boulder, CO 80306

U.S. Army Sniper Training Manual
Paladin Press
P.O. Box 1307
Boulder, CO 80306